# Pins and Pincushions

PINS AND PINCUSHIONS

"  . . Let us be content, in work,
To do the thing we can, and not presume
To fret because it's little   'Twill employ
Seven men, they say, to make a perfect pin
Who makes the head, content to miss the point ;
Who makes the point, agreed to leave the join ,
And if a man should cry, ' I want a pin,
'And I must make it straightway, head and point,'
His wisdom is not worth the pin he wants.
Seven men to a pin—and not a man too much !"

—ELIZABETH BARRETT BROWNING
*Aurora Leigh,* Book VIII.

PLATE I.

PIN-PRICKT PICTURE.

*English, date about 1710.*

# PINS AND
# PINCUSHIONS

LONGMANS, GREEN AND CO
39 PATERNOSTER ROW, LONDON
NEW YORK, BOMBAY, AND CALCUTTA
1911

# PINS AND PINCUSHIONS

BY

E. D. LONGMAN

AND

S. LOCH

THE ARMS OF THE PINNERS' COMPANY

*WITH 43 PLATES*

LONGMANS, GREEN AND CO
39 PATERNOSTER ROW, LONDON
NEW YORK, BOMBAY, AND CALCUTTA
1911

TO

# T. N. L.

*" To cultivate kindness is a great part*
*of the business of life "*—JOHNSON.

# PREFACE

A FEW words will suffice to explain that this book has been written with the view of pointing out the great importance of the " Pin," both in ancient and in modern times. It may be said that some parts of the work do not actually concern " Pins " in the usual interpretation of the word, but the authors hope their readers will find there is always good and sufficient reason for introducing each subject They trust, therefore, there is no occasion to apologise for giving to the public their humble record of the precious " Pin," in the sincere hope that what they have written may teach the world to realise its intrinsic value.

The authors are much indebted for the kind consideration of those who have enabled them to reproduce many interesting and curious things among their illustrations, and they wish particularly to thank Mr. Thomas Radcliffe, Worksop; Mr S. Cowles, the University Museum of Archæology and Ethnology at Cambridge; Mr. J. Jennings, Bassett House, Newmarket; Mrs. Head (whose works they quote), Mr. A. Pelham Trotter, Colonel Croft Lyons, Mr. A. Wynne Corrie, and Mrs. Thrale. Thanks are also due to the Dowager Lady Arundell of Wardour, to whom they owe illustrations of the famous Glastonbury Cup; Lady Sackville, who has most kindly contributed many interesting relics from Knole; the Marquis of Normanby, the Earl of Denbigh, the authorities of the British Museum, the Victoria and Albert Museum, and the Natural History Museum; Dr. Joseph Anderson, LL.D , keeper of the Museum of Antiquities, Edinburgh; Mr. Leverton Harris, M.P.; Mr. Griffiths, Bangor; Mr. Emery Walker; Mr. Walter Acton, 11A East Street, Brighton; M. Dumoulin, the publisher of *La Révolution*, by Charles D'Héricault, in which appeared the facsimile of Marie Antoinette's pin-prickt letter (see page 121); the Proprietors of *Notes and Queries*, the *Queen*, and the *Burlington Magazine*, by whose permission Plate XXIX. is reproduced, Messrs. Kirby and Beard (for information kindly given), and to many other friends, whose assistance has been of much value.

The photographs for reproduction were principally taken, for the authors, by Messrs. Searle Brothers, 191 Brompton Road. They also wish to acknowledge their indebtedness to the works of Sir John Evans, Miss Abraham (*Greek Costume*), and to Professor W. Ridgeway's *The Early Age of Greece*.

ELEANOR D LONGMAN.
SOPHY LOCH

# CONTENTS

## CHAPTER VIII

## CHAPTER IX

## CHAPTER X

## CHAPTER XI

## CHAPTER XII

# LIST OF ILLUSTRATIONS

# LIST OF ILLUSTRATIONS xiii

# PINS AND PINCUSHIONS

## CHAPTER I

### THE HISTORY OF THE PIN, FROM ANCIENT TIMES TO THE PRESENT DAY

"See that there be not a loose pin in the work of your salvation."—
RUTHERFORD, *Letter to J Gordon*, 1637.

"His garment nought but many ragged clouts,
With thornes together pined and patched was "
—SPENSER'S *Faerie Queene*, 1590.

THE history of such a universal and commonplace object as a pin (as at present known) would not seem perhaps at first sight to offer material of much interest to the general reading public, and yet we venture to think that some of the information we have been able to collect on the subject may prove of interest. "To begin from the beginning" is sometimes as much desired by grown-up readers as by children, and we therefore propose to trace the origin and evolution of the pin from ancient to modern times.

A pin is a small spike, usually made of metal, with a bulbed head or some other arrangement to prevent the spike passing entirely through the cloth or other material which it is fastening together. This is, broadly speaking, the modern definition of a pin. In one form or another pins are of the highest antiquity, and it may be assumed that their use is coeval with human dress or covering of any kind,

A

the earliest form doubtless being a natural thorn, such
as is still to be seen fastening the dresses of peasant
women in Upper Egypt. This theory would seem
to be confirmed by the word itself, which is derived
from the Latin *spina*—a thorn. *Spina Christi* is the
name of the tree on which grow the large thorns
used as pins in Egypt. In ancient times, thorns
curiously scraped and dried were called by the poor
women of Wales " Pindraen," and were probably
also used to secure their clothing. From ages past
to the present day, gipsies have used pin-thorns to pin
their tents and garments. Quite recently, Gipsy Lee
of Aldeburgh in Suffolk (aged nearly a hundred
years) wrote to her great-niece, living near Southwold
in the same county, asking her to send her some
pin-thorns, as they were not procurable in her own
neighbourhood. These pin-thorns are the long thorns
of the new shoots of the blackthorn. [They are
boiled or fried in oil or fat in order to maintain their
rigidity and also to prevent their easily snapping.
They are straightened out when cooked. Plate II.,
Illustration 1, shews one of these pin-thorns. In
one of the Asiatic countries the articles of food
bought by the poorer population are wrapped in a
big leaf, which is then secured with a thorn. Pin-
thorns are also used in the New Hebrides for many
purposes, and the Musquakie Indians (North America)
also make use of them. In Plate XLII., Illustration 2, will be seen one of a Musquakie Indian
pincushion with the thorns used by these people.

Following after the natural pin came the pins
made of bone, dating from the Prehistoric Age,
and we are much indebted to the works of Sir
John Evans, which have enabled us to classify pins

PLATE II

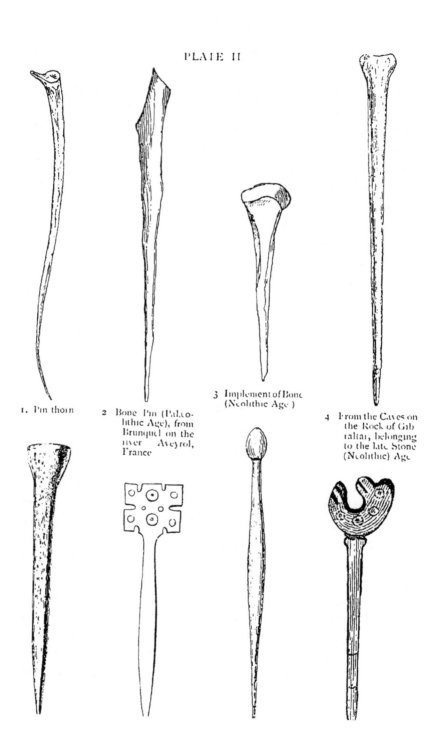

1. Pin thorn

2 Bone Pin (Palaeolithic Age), from Brunquel on the river Aveyrol, France

3 Implement of Bone (Neolithic Age)

4 From the Caves on the Rock of Gibraltar, belonging to the late Stone (Neolithic) Age

according to the different periods to which they belong. A brief description of these periods, gathered from Sir John Evans's works, may be of advantage. Reference is made particularly to the antiquities of Western Europe.

*The Iron Age* in Denmark and in all Western Europe is supposed to go back to about the Christian era.

*The Bronze Age*, to embrace a period of one or two thousand years previous to that date; and

*The Stone Age* (and Bone) all previous time of man's occupation of that part of the world.

The Stone Age has two different periods—Palæolithic and Neolithic.

The Palæolithic Period is by far the more ancient, and the objects are found in caverns, and beneath layers of stalagmite and in ancient alluvia—in both cases usually associated with the remains of animals either locally or entirely extinct.

In the Neolithic Period objects were found upon or near the surface of the soil, in encampments, on the sites of ancient habitations, and in tumuli (mounds). This period is sometimes called the Surface Period.

This classification into different ages in no way implies any exact chronology, far less one that would be applied to all the countries of Europe alike, for it is evident that at the times when, for instance, in a country such as Italy, the Iron Age may have commenced, some of the more northern countries of Europe may possibly have been in their Bronze Age, and others again still in their Stone Age. It is impossible to fix any hard and fast limits for the close of the Stone (and Bone) Period, or for the beginning or end of the Bronze Period, or for the commencement of that of Iron.

It does not follow that in the Bronze Age of any country, stone and bone instruments had entirely ceased to be in use, or even that in the Iron Age both bronze and stone had been completely superseded for all cutting purposes. Though the succession of these three stages of civilisation may here be regarded as certain, the transition from one to the other must have required a long course of years to become general, and even in any particular district the change cannot have been sudden. There must have been a time when in each district the new phase of civilisation was being introduced and the old conditions had not entirely changed.

The illustrations and descriptions of pins of different periods which are given start from the earliest times and take the reader up to the modern pin. Plate II., Illustrations 2, 3, 4, are examples, after the thorn, of the earliest known method of fastening on clothing.

These represent, of course, the pin in its rudest form, but the next illustration (5), Plate II., shews one which is better shaped and therefore no doubt more acceptable to the feminine mind of the period.

This specimen is in the Natural History Museum at South Kensington, and it will be noticed that the body of the pin is nearly circular and expands into a head, the point tapering off sharply. It is highly polished from constant use, the dress it fastened being probably made of skins. It belongs to the Palæolithic Period.

The prehistoric woman must soon have persuaded her husband that the head of the pin ought to be more of an ornamental nature, and an example is given here of a bone pin, the head of which shews some attempt at decoration (Plate II., Illustration 6).

Plate II., Illustration 7, shews a bone pin of Celtic origin found in Cambridgeshire, and Illustration 8, a pin of elegant shape, of Roman origin, found in Yorkshire. It has been most carefully fashioned, and the point is almost as finely tapered as the bronze pin seen in Plate VIII. Before passing on, it is interesting to note the curious custom in use in Egypt, of fastening down the eyelids of the dead with a very fine fish-bone.

As has been already seen, there is considerable difficulty in classifying the pins of different ages in their exact order, as the Stone, Bronze, and Iron Ages overlapped each other in different countries owing to the varying degrees of civilisation to which these countries had attained; it would therefore seem that a certain amount of latitude must be allowed in giving examples of pins in different parts of the world, and our aim has been more to give a general survey of the gradual development of the pin both as regards material and make from the earliest periods onwards, than to attempt a fully detailed chronological account, which would be beyond the scope of our present work. It may, however, be safely accepted that following after the Palæolithic and Neolithic Periods, during which the "pins" or "clothes fasteners" were made of bone from the fibula of some animal, split and then rubbed to a point—which were generally found in caves in the Palæolithic Period and in the Neolithic Period in tumuli or encampments—came the Bronze Age; that is to say, an age in which these and other implements were made of bronze, a composition metal of copper and tin. It is again very difficult sometimes to say whether bronze pins, certainly of great antiquity, belong to the Bronze Age properly so called, or to the late Celtic or early Iron Period.

The development of clothing for both sexes, rendered a more finely tapered and highly polished pin necessary, and we see this in one of the earliest examples of bronze pins (Plate III., Illustration 1), which resembles in shape the bone pin seen in Plate II., Illustration 5. This bronze pin was found near Durham.

Illustrations 2 and 3 in Plate III. are also of very simple design, but with an attempt at ornamentation, as will be seen from the double cross roughly raised on the bronze on the one, and the slightly decorated head and shank of the other.

It would seem that nothing fresh in the shape of pins of any kind has been invented since the epoch of the Bronze Age, and though fashion may be "ever changing" it is not "ever new," as will be seen from Illustration 4 in Plate II. of a very remarkable specimen of a double pin dating from that age, connected with a chain, similar to such as are in use at the present day. The evolution of the brooch from the pin is a subject full of interest, but it is not proposed to enter into it in these pages, except in so far as to speak of the primitive safety-pin, the earliest form of the brooch. These safety-pins were in full use in Northern Italy before the end of the Bronze Age, as well as several marked modifications, or, more strictly speaking, developments of the same. The birth of the safety-pin seems to have been somewhat in this wise. Long slender pins of bronze were a character-

PLATE III

1. Bronze Pin found
near Durham.

2. Bronze Pin.

3. Bronze Pin.

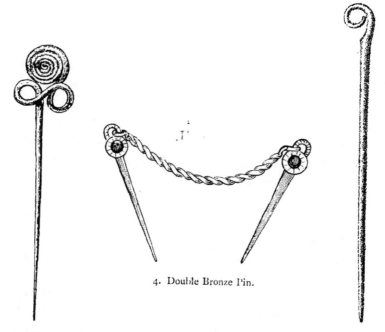

4. Double Bronze Pin.

5. Bronze Pin.  (Lake
Dwellings of Italy.)

*rom Prof. W. Ridgeway's
"The Early Age of
Greece." (Cambridge*

6. Bronze Pin.  (Lake
Dwellings of Italy.)

*From Prof. W. Ridgeway's
"The Early Age of
Greece." (Cambridge*

istic feature of the lake dwellings of Italy and those of some contiguous countries. In Illustrations 5 and 6, Plate III., are shewn two examples of this kind of pin, one simply crooked to form a head, and the other elaborated into a spiral. Evidently one day a necessity arose in some one's existence to fasten his or her body-covering with greater security than that afforded by an ordinary pin, and the "some one" conceived the idea of bending the body of the pin after passing it through the garment and securing the point behind the head. The first step taken, a second naturally followed, that of giving a complete turn to the pin, and thus getting the spring. The body of the fibula began by being straight and parallel to the pin, but this not giving room enough for the cloth of the garment it was fastening, the bow shape was adopted, the bow being first very high and semicircular in shape, and then becoming lower. The disc was originally formed by several twists of a fine round wire; the number of twists became smaller, the wire became broader and flattened, and the diameter of the disc increased. The latter then became a complete plate, the body and spring being made all of one piece like the modern safety-pin. These bow fibulæ were found in every grave, even in those of children, and the earliest types date from the fifteenth century B.C. The safety-pin went through many evolutions as regards shape and style, and also the metal of which it was composed varied much, bronze, iron, and gold being all used in its manufacture, but it is most curious and interesting to note that it is the primitive and simplest form which has survived and is still in use at the present day.

Long stiletto pins with ribbed handles have been

found in Egyptian deposits of about 1450 to 1200 B.C., and also in Cyprus and at Sparta. Very long pins, also with ribbed handles, fasten the garments of one of the figures in the François vase (now at Florence), dated by some authorities in the seventh century, but by others about 570-550 B.C. This figure is depicted wearing a garment fastened on the shoulder by pins inserted "down towards the breast." The material of which the top garment is composed is drawn from the back, and wraps over that which covers the front; the pins are then inserted downwards and hold the two thicknesses of material together. These prodigious pins were of such size and strength that they could become dangerous and even murderous weapons in the hands of excited women, and, according to Herodotus, this was actually the case when a disastrous expedition was undertaken by the Athenians during the first half of the sixth century. One man only returned alive to Athens, and the story goes that the wives of those who had fallen in battle were so infuriated with the unfortunate man for having escaped when their husbands had perished, that they killed him with the brooches and pins with which their dresses were fastened, asking him as they stabbed him where he had left their husbands. This somewhat illogical conduct on the part of the Athenian women led to a different style of dress being imposed upon them which did not need these large pins, but was secured on the body by being sewn on the shoulders. The upper part of the sleeve was also sewn together or fastened by a number of small brooches. According to some authorities, these sewn garments were a reversion to a former fashion two or three centuries earlier.

PLATE IV

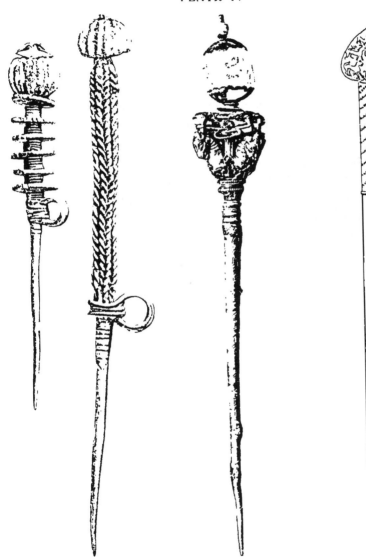

1  Two Gold Hairpins

(*About the 8th century B C
found at Salamis in
Cyprus*)

2  Gold Pin  (Size, 6¾ in
long )

(*About the 7th century B C
found at Chiusi in
Tuscany*)

3  Votive  Hairpin  of
Gold,  surmounted
with a Pearl, dedi-
cated to Aphrodite
(Size, 8 in. long )

(*About the 6th century B C
From the Temple of
Aphrodite at Paphos
in Cyprus*)

Pins for the hair have been generally used by women in all ages, and even men wore them when the fashion of allowing their hair to grow long made it necessary to arrange it in the same way as the women. This fashion is supposed to have had its birth in Asia, from whence it made its way into other parts of the world. The hairpin consisted of a single pin with an ornamental head, and it is somewhat difficult to differentiate between a pin worn in the hair and a pin to fasten clothing; possibly the distinction is not very great. Illustration 1 (Plate IV.) shews two beautiful pins of the Homeric age, about the eighth century B.C. They are made of gold, and were found at Salamis in Cyprus. They are now in the British Museum. The loop at the side is probably for some form of attachment (possibly a gold chain was affixed), and it would seem from their general appearance these handsome pins may have been designed for hair ornaments. It would also seem reasonable to suppose that in this category would also be included a beautiful gold pin found at Chiusi in Tuscany, dating, it is supposed, from the seventh century B.C. It is decorated with circles placed one over the other (Plate IV., Illustration 2).

The Athenians who called themselves Autochtones (the original inhabitants of a country who are the first possessors of it and never have mingled with other nations) wore grasshoppers in their hair as a symbol of their antiquity, for they thought that this insect was directly engendered from the earth. They abandoned this custom about the time of the wars of the Medes and Persians.

Illustration 3 (Plate IV.) is a votive hairpin of gold surmounted by a pearl, and inscribed with a dedication to Aphrodite (from Temple of Aphrodite at Paphos in Cyprus, about sixth century B.C.). In the category of highly ornamental hairpins would also be included the three next illustrations (Plate V.), all of which are made of silver, and are in the Louvre Museum in Paris.

Illustration 1 represents a hand of Venus or Paris holding an apple.

Illustration 2 shews a magnificent pin, the head of which is composed of lentils placed one above the other, slightly engraved, through which passes the stem; on the top is a kind of drum which holds a boar's head.

Illustration 3 is in the same style, with a ram's head.

When the hairpin (sometimes termed a bodkin, and by the Saxons a hair-needle) became a "biped" must have been, we venture to think, when the fashion came in of wearing the hair in curls close to the head, as it would be well-nigh impossible without terrible loss of time and temper to keep the curls in place with a single pin.

For ornamental pins all kinds of metals, as we have seen, were brought into requisition, as well as ivory and bone, and a beautiful specimen of a Saxon pin is shewn in Illustration 1 (Plate VI.). The shank is made of brass with the head of gold, ornamented with red and blue stones and filigree work, and was probably used for the hair and for fastening the mantle.

Another very decorative Saxon pin is seen in Illustration 2 (Plate VI.); it is made of bronze, with a gold head, ornamented with garnets and pearls.

Hairpins of a somewhat humbler kind made of

PLATE V

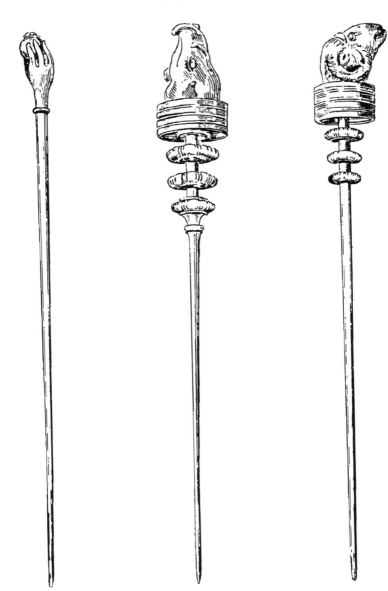

1  Silver Hairpin with Hand
   holding an Apple  (Size,
   6¾ in long )

2  Silver Hairpin with Boar's
   Head  (Size,  6¾ in
   long )

3  Silver Hairpin with Ra
   Head  (Size,  6¾
   long )

( The Louvre Museum, Paris )

PLATE VI

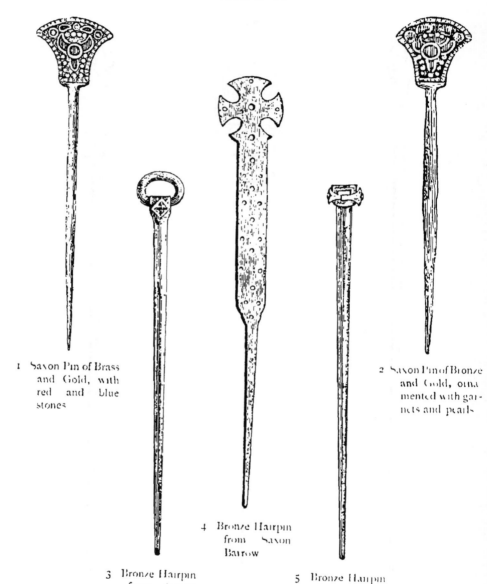

1 Saxon Pin of Brass and Gold, with red and blue stones

2 Saxon Pin of Bronze and Gold, ornamented with garnets and pearls

3 Bronze Hairpin from Saxon Barrow

4 Bronze Hairpin from Saxon Barrow

5 Bronze Hairpin from Saxon Barrow

PLATE VII

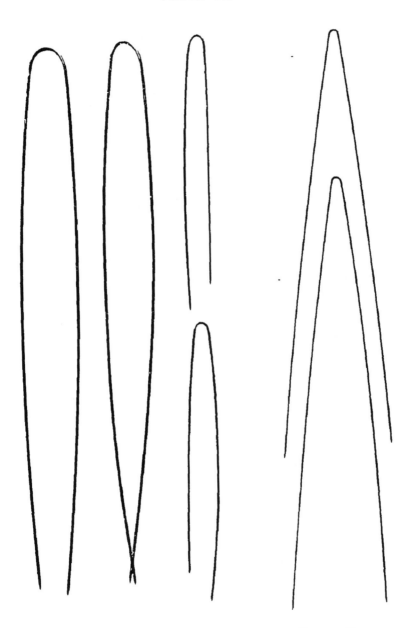

Hairpins of the Jacobite Period.
(Sizes, 7½ in. and 4½ in. long.)

Georgian Hairpins
(Size, 10¼ in. long.)

bronze have been found in England in Saxon barrows.
They are shewn in Illustrations 3, 4, 5 (Plate VI.).

The shape, or rather shapes of the modern hairpin
(for there are many varieties) are doubtless familiar
to all, but the illustration of the Jacobite and later
Georgian hairpins are interesting (Plate VII.). They
are curiously " straddle-legged," and it will be noticed
one end is longer, as a rule, than the other. The
Georgian hairpins are the largest, and their prodigious
size was rendered necessary by the enormous erections
of powdered hair in vogue at that time.

Pins are mentioned in the Bible, but the Hebrew
word specially refers to tent-pins, and is frequently
used in connection with tents, and with the Jewish
tabernacle in particular. Pins (nails or stakes) were
used for holding together the different parts of this
tent. There are many allusions to these in Exodus.
" All the vessels of the tabernacle, in all the service
thereof, and all the pins thereof, and all the pins of the
court, shall be of brass " (Exodus xxvii. 19, A.V.).
It is thought by some that the brass mentioned in
the Scriptures should be understood as having reference to copper, either in its pure state or as alloyed
with tin, rather than to any compound exactly answer-
ing to our brass. There are further references in
Exodus and Numbers to pins, meaning pins which
fastened or made fast different parts of the tabernacle
and which were made of " brass," but the tent-pins to
which the ropes of the tents were fastened were (it
is thought) fashioned of wood, as amongst the Be-
douins of the present day. The instrument recorded
as having been driven by Jael through Sisera's temple,
some think was a stake, or tent-pin. The pin which
fastened the web (into which Delilah had woven

Samson's hair) was the batten or pin with which the woof is beaten up into the web (Judges xvi. 14): "And she fastened it with the pin, and said unto him, The Philistines be upon thee, Samson. And he awaked out of his sleep, and went away with the pin of the beam, and with the web." In Ezekiel xv. 3 the word pin is used for a peg for hanging up any vessel.

In Isaiah xxii. 33 and Ezra ix. 8 it is used as typical of great security and strength: "I will fasten him as a nail in a sure place," and "to give us a nail in His holy place."

The large pins or nails used in erecting an Eastern house being built into the wall, or fixed very securely, the expression in these verses pictures a secure position, a constant and sure abode. The pin is therefore here typical of great strength, and as it secures the different parts of an Eastern house, so Ezra, mourning for the wickedness of the Jewish people and praying for their reformation, asks God to give them as secure and safe an abode (from sin) as is given by the pin in an Eastern house. In Zechariah x. 4 the word is figuratively used to signify a ruler, or support of the State. Crisping-pins, which we may suppose to be curling-pins, are mentioned in Isaiah iii. 22: "The Lord will take away . . . the mantles, the whimples, and the crisping-pins."

Before leaving the subject of pins or nails used in holding together different parts of a house, it will be interesting to our readers to note Illustration 1 (Plate VIII.), which represents the pin which fell from the roof of Westminster Hall, where it was used as a wooden nail or pin to keep some part of the woodwork together. Wooden pins are used at the present time for boat-building.

PLATE VIII

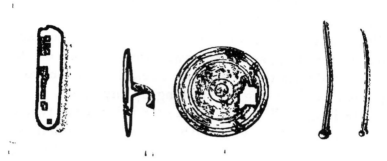

1 Wooden Pin from the roof of Westminster Hall

7. Bronze Pin found at Edinburgh

4 Two Saxon Bronze Pins from Aldeburgh in Suffolk

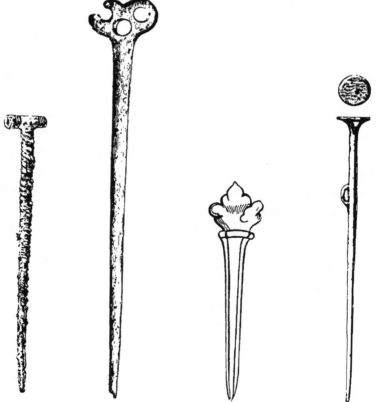

2 Pin of Twisted Bronze found in English

3 Bronze Pin found in an interment in

5 Pin represented fastening the shroud of John Stretford, Archbishop of Can-

6 Irish flat headed Pin made of bronze

PLATE IX

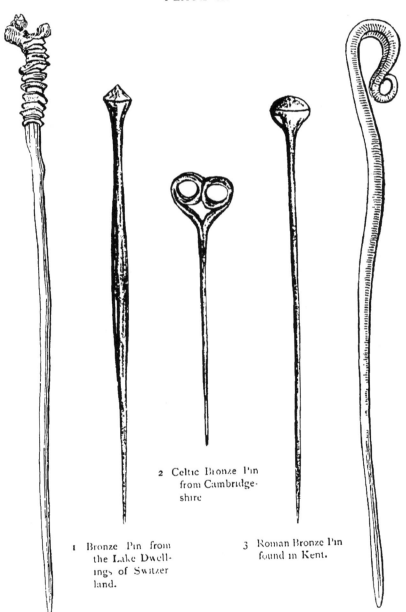

2 Celtic Bronze Pin
from Cambridge-
shire

1 Bronze Pin from
the Lake Dwell-
ings of Switzer
land.

3 Roman Bronze Pin
found in Kent.

Bronze Pin from
Saxony

5 Bronze Pin from
Kiev, in South
Russia

Pins or skewers of bone are constantly found in British barrows, both with burnt and unburnt bodies, and also on the site of human occupation, some with perforated ends and some without. They may have been used to fasten some kind of shroud or to pin a cloth in which the ashes of the deceased were placed after being collected from the funeral pile. Bronze pins are also found in barrows as well as those made of bone. Illustration 2 (Plate VIII.) represents a pin of twisted bronze found in a barrow in England with burnt bones  The pin is six inches long, in the form of a crutch, with a perforated head.

Illustration 3 (Plate VIII.) shews a pin (four and a half inches) found in an interment in Wales, near Carnarvon. It has a bi-loped head and three perforations.

The two bronze pins in Illustration 4 (Plate VIII.) were recently found at Aldeburgh in Suffolk. They were washed up by a devastating high tide which flowed over a Saxon burying-ground. In Orford Church near by there is a brass which shews how the shrouds of the dead were pinned on with such pins.

It may be mentioned here that the pinning of the shroud or covering of the dead seems to have been in use many centuries later, as Illustration 5 (Plate IX.) shews the pin which is represented fastening the pall of John Stratford, Archbishop of Canterbury, who died in 1348. His effigy is in the cloisters of Canterbury Cathedral. We also note that in the statue of Isabeau de Bavière in the Abbey Church of St. Denis nearly a century later (about 1425), large pins are portrayed as fastening some of the draperies.

In Illustration 6 (Plate VIII.) is shewn an Irish example of a flat-headed bronze pin, with a small loop at the side. By some authorities it is thought that in the remains of wire which have been found attached to these loops in similar pins found in Central and Northern Europe, may be traced the embryo of the spring of the fibula, but we do not ourselves incline to this belief. This Irish pin was supposed at one time to have been of greater length.

The pin shewn in Illustration 7 (Plate VIII.) was found at Edinburgh, and is of a different type. It has an expanded head turned over so as to be on the same plane as the pin and be visible when stuck into a garment. Pins of this type belong to the later part of the Bronze Period.

Illustration 1 (Plate IX.) shews a beautiful specimen of a bronze pin from the lake dwellings of Switzerland. Its graceful shape is particularly pleasing. The rarity of bronze pins in the British Isles, especially in England, as compared with their abundance in the lake dwellings of Southern Europe, is very remarkable, as also a scarcity of bracelets and other ornaments, and it is conjectured by some authorities that the jet and amber which were so much in fashion for ornaments during our Bronze Age suited the native taste better than metal which was used for tools and weapons.

Illustration 2 (Plate IX.) represents a Celtic bronze pin from Cambridgeshire, and Illustration 3 a beautifully shaped Roman pin with a fine and tapering point. This latter pin was found in Kent.

Two more specimens of bronze pins are shewn in Illustrations 4 and 5 (Plate IX.). One is from Saxony, and the other from Kiev in South Russia. The Russian one much resembles the class of bronze pins from which the safety-pins were evolved.

Almost every variety of jewellery has been found in

PLATE X

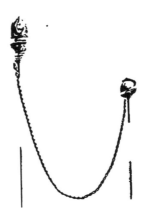

1  Breast-pin found
at Pompeii

2  Double Breast-pin of Gold and
Coral, which belonged to John
Frederick Sackville, third Duke
of Dorset

3  Pin-maker's Peg, made of bone

4  The kind of Pin which was filed on the Peg

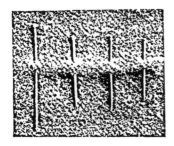

6  Round-headed Pin
*Date,* 1570

the ruins of Pompeii and Herculaneum, and Illustration 1 (Plate X.) shews quite a different class of pin from any previously spoken of. It represents a breast-pin on which considerable artistic ingenuity has been lavished. It was found in the excavations at Pompeii, and consists of a bacchanalian figure holding a glass in one hand and in the other a patera or open vessel approaching to the form of a cup, used by the Greeks and Romans in their sacrifices and libations. He is provided with bat's wings, emblematic of the drowsiness consequent on hard drinking, and two bands of grapes pass across his body.

We will now turn to comparatively modern times. Some authorities think that pins more or less in their present form (though probably coarser) were used in France before they made their appearance in England, but however that may be, we find them in full use in the former country in the first half of the fourteenth century. Some of them were very long, and must have been used for the hair. The fashion then in use among the ladies of wearing veils, whimples (a habit-shirt fastened round the neck and bust), stomachers, lappets, kerchiefs, and horns, required quantities of pins, and it was by means of small brooches made of wire that these headgears were fixed on the head and fastened round the throat.

This appears to have much exercised a contemporary writer, Jehan de Mohun, as he protests in the *Roman de la Rose* against the encroachments of fashion to secure these furbelows on the head and to fasten them round the neck.

"About half a dishful of pins are stuck about the horns and round the whimple." Then he adds: "Par Dieu! Many times has my heart been wrung to see a lady so securely tied up that her whimple seemed nailed to her neck, or that the pins are stuck in her flesh." And he goes on: "One must not admire their fastenings too close, for they sting worse than nettles or thistles." This is reminiscent of the story (told by himself) of Pepys and the pretty girl in church. No doubt it will be remembered by all: how Pepys, attending divine service one day, did perceive a very pretty girl in the congregation whose acquaintance he desired to make. He accordingly made his way towards her, doubtless wishful to put his arm around her, but she (evidently not caring for his advances) did "out with a pin," which effectually cooled Pepys's ardour.

In 1347, 12,000 pins were delivered from the royal wardrobe for one of the French princesses, and in 1400 the Duchess of Orleans purchased of Jehan de Bréconnier, épinglier of Paris, several thousand long and short pins, besides 500 "de la façon d'Angleterre." So that pins appear not only to have been manufactured in England, but to have been of high repute even in the reign of Henry IV. (1399-1413). This theory is borne out by the records of the Pinmakers' Company, of which more presently. Some authorities would, however, have us believe that the ladies in England were content to fasten their garments with skewers of gold, silver, brass, iron, or bone (some with ornamental heads), while the French ladies were using more delicate accessories to the toilet; but if this was the case it was only by a few years that France was ahead of England in this respect. The actual date when the ordinary domestic pin came into general use in England is uncertain, but the Pinners, or Company of Pin-makers, were evidently an important body from very early days in England, as in 1376 they returned two men to the Common Council of London, and in 1469 supplied twenty men to the City Watch. The arms of the Company are seen on the title page. In the latter part of this century (fifteenth) pins were imported into this country from France in large numbers, and had become an article of sufficient importance to warrant legislative notice, as in 1483 the importation of pins was prohibited by statute. Apparently little attention, however, was paid to this, as in 1540 Queen Catherine Howard received pins from France, and Stow says in the *Antiquary's Portfolio*, "This minute implement was thought sufficiently important to merit a parliamentary legislation. Accordingly, by Statute 37, Henry VIII. cap. 13, all 'pinnes' are prohibited from being sold, unless they be 'double-headed' and the heads soldered fast to the shank of the pinne, well smoothed, the shank well shaven, the point well and round filed, cauted, and sharpened." This Act was rendered necessary, as the imported pins were often of an inferior make and their heads had an uncomfortable habit of becoming loose.

Hazlitt tells us in the book of the Livery Companies of the City of London, that the Pinners and Wire-workers, who had been one body at least since the time of Edward IV. and kept their accounts together, were united with the Girdlers in Elizabeth's reign by a charter granted to that body. In 1598 there appears to have been a depression in the industry, as the Association abandoned its Hall in Addle Street and removed elsewhere. The foreign importation of pins apparently increased instead of diminished, but the Pin-makers do not seem to have relinquished their privileges without a struggle and many bitter protests, and the presentation of many petitions to the authorities to protect them from the encroachment of the foreign producer, as we find from the following interesting petition made by the Pin-makers to Lord Burghley. It is given here *in extenso*.—

To the Right Honourable the Lord Burghley, Lord High Treasurer of England.

"Your Lordship's godly care of the common wealth encourageth your humble supplicants, the Pinners and Needlemakers of the City of London, to pray your honourable ayde for restraint of foreign wares—pins and needles. The bringing in whereof is the cause that so many idle persons perish and miscarry for want of work.

"Now in foreign lands the poor are so provided for, as the hospitals there find unto them meat, drink, and clothing, and the Artists have their works only for instructing them.

"And in this land (now that there is not such provision for the poor) your supplicants using that trade cannot live to sell their wares at so low rate as foreign wares are sold.

"But if they were restrained, many thousands should be daily sett on work and made common wealths men that now die in the streets.

"The Premisses considered and for that there are above forty thousand pounds worth of pins and needles yearly brought into the realm which are nothing so good or well wrought as those are which are made and brought within the land.

"And the restraint of bringing them in will be the

means of setting many thousands of our poor on work.

"Now that lame soldiers and children, though they have not legs, may work on that trade, may it therefore please your Lordship to give your furtherance for revising a statute for restraint of foreign wares of 3 Ed. 4, 4 (1 B. 3, 12), 5 El. 7 (14 El. 11). And your suppliants according to their most bounden duties will continually pray for your Lordship's preservation in health and increase of honour."

History repeats itself, and this quaint and interesting petition might have been written at the present time, so aptly does it describe the position to-day of many industries in England.

In the reign of James I. the foreign trade in pins was so large that it is said £60,000 a year left the country to pay for our imports, but in the last year of his reign, in 1625, the first pin manufactory of any size in England was founded by one John Tilsby in Gloucestershire, which county was long celebrated for its pins. In the reign of Charles I. in 1636 the Pinners, after existing for three centuries, perhaps by prescription, or as a subordinate member of other bodies, obtained separate letters-patent of incorporation; the home manufacture of pins began to grow more extensive and regular, and to supersede the foreign trade. Very little is heard or known, however, of the Pin-makers after their incorporation, and the combined influence of the bodies interested in keeping pins under normal mercantile control was very strong. The Pinners' or Pin-makers' Company sank more or less into oblivion, the retail business of providing pins being, however, one of the lucrative specialities of the haberdashers of smallwares.

The trade found its way to Bristol and Birmingham, at which latter place, in connection with a previously established wire-work, it became localised. The pin was then "wire-headed," and fourteen or fifteen people were necessary for the processes required, and the numerous details connected with the common pin were seized on later by Adam Smith as one of the most remarkable illustrations of the advantages of the division of labour.

Metal pins were very expensive luxuries for some time after they first made their appearance in their present form, owing no doubt to the great amount of hand labour involved in the making, and in consequence they were very acceptable as New Year's gifts to ladies, and money given for the purchase of them was called "pin-money," an expression which was further extended to a sum of money secured by a husband on his marriage for the expenses of his wife's wardrobe and adornment. There was an ancient tax in France for providing the Queen with pins, which also may have led to the adoption of this term. The makers of the pins were allowed to sell them in open shops only on January 1st and 2nd, when the Court ladies and city dames flocked to the depôts to buy them. We find from the household accounts of Katherine, Countess of Devon, 1524, that in the sixteenth century the price of pins was as follows :—

"Necessaries for my lady . . . a pin case, 16d. . . . 1000 white pins, 8d . . . ditto black, 7d." In the State calendars in the reign of Henry VIII., 1524, from accounts of revels held December 29th, 16th of Henry VIII., we learn that for 1 oz. ribands for hair laces, 11d. was given, and for laton pins, 8d. The silver penny of this period was (approximately) equal in value to $3\frac{1}{10}$ present pence.

John Huser the younger, when writing to Lady Lisle at Calais in 1534, says, "I am sending by Nicholas of the Hall 2 oz. of ribbon . . . and 2000 pins."

The cost of pins was lessened in 1560. Those of the best quality were made of brass, superseding the iron pin to a great extent, but pins of iron wire blanched were often passed off as brass pins. At this present time pins made of brass are the best for all general purposes, but for use in delicate materials, those made from steel wire are more suitable, as the steel being harder than brass, the pins can be made finer and stronger, and do not make so large a hole as brass and iron pins. Many of the pretty French hatpins on the market are supplied with their steel stems by English firms.

The pin of the present day varies very much, not only in size but in excellence. But there is a general consensus of opinion that the English pin is one of the best, if not *the* best the world produces. This has more or less always been recognised, and more than one hundred and thirty years ago in America, in 1775, the Congress of America offered a premium in that year of £50 for the first twenty-five dozen of domestic pins equal to those imported from England.

The beautiful automatic machinery by which pins are now made of lengths of wire is an invention of the early part of the nineteenth century. In 1817, a machine for producing pins with "head, shaft, and point in one entire piece" was invented by Seth Hunt, an American, thus realising a "solid-headed" pin.

This ingenious machine was purchased in 1818 by the well-known firm of Kirby, Beard & Co., but does not appear to have been a success, and was not taken into general use. For some years after this attempt to introduce machinery, the old processes of hand manufacture were continued, and no improvements took place of much magnitude.

In 1824, Mr. Samuel Wright of Massachusetts patented a pin-making machine in England, but it fell to the old English firm of world-wide renown, already referred to, to be the pioneers in England of machine-made pins. This was in 1833, and, a little later on, a machine was invented for making pins with solid heads direct from wire. The process by which this is done is most interesting, the accuracy and speed of the machine being quite wonderful, and pins pointed and provided with heads are now produced at the rate of 180 to 220 per minute. The consumption of pins in Great Britain is now computed at several millions daily.

Illustration 2 (Plate X.) is a beautiful example of a double gold pin, the large pin a little more than three inches long, and the smaller pin two inches long. The heads are of coral, and the two pins are connected by a gold chain three inches in length. The head of the larger pin is ornamented with a gold serpent having eyes of rubies and a diamond on its forehead. Pins of this description have been used during many epochs of the world's history, and our readers will remember the double bronze pin dating from the Bronze Age shewn them in Illustration 4 (Plate III.). This more modern specimen belonged to John Frederick Sackville, third Duke of Dorset, and was doubtless used to fasten the neck-cloth or cravat.

PLATE XI

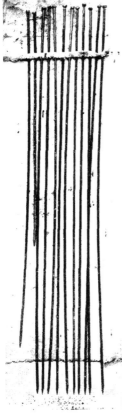

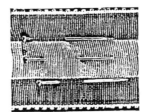

3. Pins on old ribbon dating back to beginning of 19th century.

1. Pins dating back to the Jacobite Rising in 1745. (Size, 7½ in.)

               a

               b

               c

4. Three lace Pins—(a) used in torchon lace-making; (b) in Buckinghamshire lace; (c) in Honiton lace.

2. Pin of later Georgian date.

5. Lilliputian Pins more than fifty years old.

Illustration 3 (Plate X.) is very interesting, and represents a pin-maker's peg. This peg is made of bone, and is in the University Museum at Cambridge. The brass wire was placed in the grooves indicated in the illustration in order that the points might be filed. The marks of the file on the bone are still visible. The next illustration (4), Plate X., shews the kind of pin that was filed on the peg. The head of the larger pin is interesting, and illustrates very clearly the globular head of twisted wire made separately and secured to the shank.

The four old pins shewn in Illustration 5 (Plate X.) are very curious. If the stem is taken between the finger and the thumb and twirled round whilst in that position, the stems seem to partly revolve, and disclose markings which are not apparent at first glance, or when *not* twirled. They are double-headed pins, date unknown.

Illustration 6 (Plate X.) represents a round-headed pin, which was found fastening a MS. dated 1570

Illustration 7 (Plate X.) is a brass round-headed pin from Scotland, date unknown. The two next illustrations belong to the Georgian period The long pins (Illustration 1, Plate XI.) date back to the time of the Jacobite rising in 1745, and the smaller one (2), (Plate XI.) to a little later date.

Illustration 3 (Plate XI.) shews three old double-headed pins, stuck in a piece of ribbon of the same period, dating from the beginning of the nineteenth century, or a little earlier. They belonged to Margaret Owen, heiress of Penrhos, Anglesey, born 1742, married 1763 to Sir John Stanley of Alderley.

Illustration 4 (Plate XI) shews three pins used in bobbin lace-making—(*a*) is an example of those used in torchon lace-making, (*b*) in Buckinghamshire lace, and (*c*) in Honiton lace.

Pins of the present day vary greatly in size, from the blanket pin, three inches long, to the tiny article, called Lilliputian pins, or more commonly "Lills," shown in Illustration 5 (Plate XI ). These pins are more than fifty years old. Those produced in the immediate present are still smaller, though perhaps not of quite so fine a make.

Having traced the history of the pin itself from the beginning to the present time, we would now wish to speak of another aspect of this small implement which proves how well this minute article has kept itself to the front in the history of the world.

# CHAPTER II

## CONCERNING THE IMPORTANCE OF PINS—THEIR CONNECTION WITH WITCHCRAFT—THE WAX OR CLAY MANIKIN—VARIOUS SUPERSTITIONS AND CHARMS

" Beware of Tituba    I pinch the children ;
Make little poppets and stick pins in them,
And then the children cry out they are pricked "
—LONGFELLOW, *Giles Corey of the Salem Farms*, Act v sc. 1.

THE stories and superstitions connected with pins must now engage our attention ; they are of great interest and full of inexhaustible revelations, some of which breathe the enchantment of fairy lore, and would require a greater power of words than we possess to relate their numerous fascinations with the full justice they deserve.   But pins having become in their modern form so entirely part of our lives, we accept them without a thought of their real value, or of what we should do without them ; it is therefore naturally difficult to realise the very important part they play, and have played for hundreds of years, in the drama of life.   This we hope to prove to the world, and thus awaken a greater reverence for the modern pin.   An endless variety of quaint old customs, stories, and superstitions are linked with their earliest existence as articles of daily necessity.   They were much used for magical purposes, for purposes of revenge, for enchantments in all parts of the world, and were generally considered to be a protection against witches and all kinds of evil spirits.

However, before dwelling further upon these more romantic aspects of the pin, let us turn to its practical uses, believing it to be clearly understood that many things are called pins merely because they hold together and make fast different parts of different things; of these we may mention the belaying-pin. This is a strong pin fixed in the side of a vessel, or by the mast, around which ropes are wound when they are fastened or belayed. Little iron bolts (also on vessels) by which capstan bars are held in their places in the drumhead holes are called capstan or safety pins. In 1489 we hear of " pinnes of woods to ioine the palys " (*Faytes of Armes and Chyvalrye*, II. xxiv.). In 1664 Oak is said to be " excellent for . . . pinns and peggs for tyling," *i.e.* to fasten the tiles to the roof (Evelyn, *Sylva*, p. 27). It is also part of a mechanism to convey or check motion, as, for instance, " a catch at the end of an iron pin, which prevented the pin, when passed through a slit, from repassing." A pin is also used to hang something upon—" the keys were hung upon a pin in the hall " (*Ellwood Autobiography* (1765), p. 98). The pin on which the keys were hung, held them to the wall just in the same way as the one a lady would use to pin a bow to her dress; both hold two things together, although the pin which held the keys may have been a rough piece of wood or iron, and quite different to the pins we are accustomed to take from our pincushions, and which with many people are the beginning and end of pins in general; with, of course, the exception of hairpins, hatpins, scarfpins, and safety-pins. The word " pin " is constantly used in conjunction with other things, such as "pin-money," for instance, to which reference has already been made in Chapter I.

Every one has heard of pin-money, but perhaps not every one of pin-wells, pin-cups, pin-pictures, pin-games, pin-baskets, a pin of beer, a merry-pin, a tirling-pin, &c. &c., the meaning and uses of all of which we hope shortly to explain.

When these terms were familiar to all, pins were, of course, of much greater value than they are now. But as time passed and they became cheaper and more plentiful, many of the old stories and superstitions connected with them naturally died out. Many, however, still remain. People at the present day may be heard to remark, "I don't care a pin" for this, that, or the other; "You might have heard a pin fall"; "He is not worth a pin"—which remarks show plainly how common they have become. But though they are so common, and those most frequently used of no money value, we could hardly get on without them; and if there were suddenly to be a pin famine, we should no doubt cry out, "My kingdom for a pin," as did King Richard for a horse.

Let our readers just consider for a moment what one day in their lives would be without a pin of any kind, and they will perhaps turn with greater interest to the wonderful things we shall presently relate concerning them.

There are many curious superstitions about pins, and we think the magical use of pins merits more attention than has hitherto been given to the subject. Of all superstitions it is the most widely spread, and the one most firmly fixed in the minds of our ignorant and poor to this day, though the enthusiastic faith of olden times has now passed away. That this faith was deeply rooted we cannot for one moment doubt; it must have been, to survive as it does in this matter-of-fact and realistic age. There are people living who will not start on a journey on Friday, do important business on that day, or even, it is said, take physic. Others will not sit in a room lit by three candles, will never use a black pin, or form one of a party of thirteen at dinner. Sixty or seventy years ago, not only these, but hundreds of other superstitions were still quite common.

The superstition of witchcraft stretches back into remote antiquity, and has many roots; it is universally spread throughout the different races of which the whole world is composed, and for this reason those who study the history of that remarkable time when witches and witchcraft flourished, will realise that belief in the supernatural was indeed deeply rooted, and that therefore it is not surprising some fragments still remain to hover round our lives.

Witches were associated with many of the pin superstitions; we all know that a witch was a person who had acquired supernatural power by entering into compact with evil spirits. She was decidedly an individual to be avoided; the misfortunes she produced were endless. She could punish her enemies in a variety of ways, destroy health, and cause terrible diseases by a glance of her evil eye. But when the tide turned and the trials and persecutions of witches began, it is proved that however horrible was the evil, the punishments were often unjust and hardly less terrible. For a female to be old and ill-favoured in those days was to live in positive peril. Any one might say she was a witch and expose her life to danger. The year 1682 saw the end of executions for witchcraft, and in

1736 the laws against it were formally repealed in
England. The cessation of judicial proceedings did
not, however, at once put an end to popular outrages
on supposed witches. Far from it. In 1751 an aged
female pauper was killed by a mob at Tring in Herts,
and not longer ago than 1863 a reputed wizard was
drowned in a pond at the village of Headingham in
Essex. There is a man still living in Suffolk who remembers, when a boy, seeing people trying to drown an
old man of the name of Stebbings, who was called " The
Wizard," in a pond called the Grimmer on Wickham
Skeith Green. The pond was used as a ducking-pond
for witches. From some cause or other Stebbings would
not drown; when they pressed his feet down in the
water his head popped up, and when they got his head
down then his feet would rise; so, after several attempts
to drown the poor old fellow, they gave it up in
despair and allowed him to come ashore. After this
not much faith was placed in Stebbings' supernatural
powers. In order to test them, several boys stole his
apples; and as he failed to discover the thieves, he
lost his reputation, and people ceased to employ him
to reveal mysteries.

Only a few years ago a woman who was dying in
North Wales had a prickly hedge of thorns erected round
her bed to keep off evil spirits. And in many parts
of England to this day, if a woman has the reputation
of being a witch, though she may not be ducked or
pricked with pins, she is often mobbed and jeered at,
or universally shunned.

It is also whispered that not more than twelve or
fourteen years ago a woman was roasted to death by her
husband in the west of Ireland because he believed
her to be a witch. This seems incredible, but the

old beliefs die slowly, and in many places cannot, even in these enlightened days, be regarded entirely as creations of fancy. Therefore, when we consider the utter ignorance and dark superstition of those mediæval days, when the belief in witches and witchcraft was a kind of religion, we can hardly be surprised at the power with which this faith then ruled mankind, and it seems only natural that precautions should have been taken, and antidotes sought for, as a protection against them.

It has already been said that pins were much used for this purpose, probably because being pointed instruments they could easily injure or hurt, and one way of proving a woman to be a witch who was suspected of being one, was to prick her with pins. A pin was inserted into various parts of her body, to see if she had that partial insensibility to pain which was understood to be an undoubted proof of the witch quality.

Pins were also used as charms for the prevention and cure of various diseases, to keep off bad dreams, to prevent ill-luck, to bring good luck, besides wounding one's enemies. A piece of bacon stuck full of pins was sometimes hung in a chimney to intercept witches in their descent and so prevent their visit. In Scotland stockings were hung crossways at the foot of the bed with a pin stuck in them to keep off the nightmare. It was also believed that pins would cure warts, and one way of doing this was to make the sign of a cross on each wart with a pin, and then throw it away. There is an old woman now living in Suffolk who cures warts in this way.

In Somersetshire it is believed that ague can be cured by getting a large spider and putting it in a box. The ague will disappear as the spider starves, and when it is dead will leave the patient entirely. This is evidently a remnant of the old orthodox waxen manikin stuck full of pins, which, some sixty years ago, was still much in use for purposes of revenge. The Flemings called dwarfs "menikin"; from which, no doubt, our term "manikin" comes, and "minikin" (small pins). The wax or clay image called the manikin was supposed to represent the one to whom you wished ill, and by piercing the image with pins, whoever it represented was supposed also to be pierced. For the charm to take proper effect, the name of the person to be injured should be written upon the breast of the image. Lord Avebury, citing Dubois, tells us the manikin superstition existed in India, only thorns were used instead of pins as piercing instruments.

This experiment was practised in all parts of the world, and is one of the commonest criminal acts recorded of magicians.

There was a plot to kill Rameses III. in this way, and other instances from the Chaldean tablets, as well as from the Babylonian and Assyrian inscriptions generally. Horace mentions these dolls; and Medea and other enchantresses made use of them. In the reign of Charles IX. of France such images were found in the house of La Mole, and it was said that he procured them in order to accomplish the death of Charles, then labouring under a mortal disease. He was condemned for having them, and suffered death on the scaffold.

Longfellow's play, *Giles Corey of the Salem Farms,* is founded on the witchcraft superstitions of the New

England States.  The scene is Salem in 1692.  In
Act iii. sc. 2 we find the following passage :—

> " What most convinced me of the woman's guilt
> Was finding hidden in her cellar wall
> Those poppets made of rags, with headless pins
> Stuck into them point outwards "

The Duchess of Gloucester's endeavour to kill
Henry VI., whether the story be true or false, has
found a place in history.  We are also told that the life
of Pope Urban VI was attempted in a similar manner.
The practice is heard of at Inverness in the earlier
part of the eighteenth century, and similar acts of
" perfidy " were practised at a much later time among
the North American Indians.  In 1677 Sir George
Maxwell of Pollok is said to have been bewitched
and tormented by means of waxen and clay images,
the pins in which, we are told, had been put there
by the devil himself.  From *The Diary of a Lady-
in-Waiting*, by Lady Charlotte Bury, we learn that
" unhappy Queen Caroline, when Princess of Wales,
was extremely outspoken to correspondents regarding
her husband.  'The only astonishing news I can offer
you,' writes the Princess on one occasion, 'is that the
Regent is dangerously ill; still, I am not sanguine
enough to flatter myself that the period to all my
troubles and misfortunes is yet to come.  Yet one
must hope for the best.' "  " After dinner," writes
Lady Charlotte Bury on another occasion, " her Royal
Highness made a wax figure as usual and gave it an
amiable addition of large horns ; then took three pins
out of her garment and stuck them through and
through, and put the figure to roast and melt at
the fire.  If it was not too melancholy to have

PLATE XII

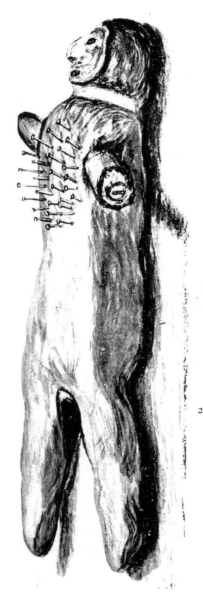

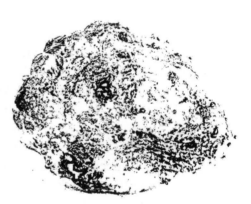

2. Calf's Heart stuck full of Pins.  (Size, 3¾ in. × 3 in.)

*From a Specimen in the National Museum of
Antiquities, Edinburgh.*

Clay Model of a Human Figure called
"Corp Chreadh."  (Size, 8¼ in. long.)

*From a Specimen in the University Museum
of Archæology and Ethnology, Cambridge.*

to do with this, I could have died of laughing.
Lady ——— says the Princess indulges in this amusement whenever there are no strangers at table; and
she thinks her Royal Highness really has a superstitious belief that destroying this effigy of her husband will bring to pass the destruction of his royal
person."

An interesting link with the past has only lately
been severed, by the death of an old man in Somersetshire who was well acquainted with the use of the wax
doll, and had known people who, having a deep grudge
against some one, really made wax dolls, stuck them
with pins and placed them near the fire to melt, believ-
ng the victims they represented would waste away also.

A story is told of a certain vice-chancellor of the
'Jniversity of Cambridge who prohibited a play.
This led to an undergraduate making a clay figure
of the offending dignitary and sticking it full of
pins. It is said the vice-chancellor had a bad attack
of the gout afterwards!

In Wales a toad sometimes took the place of the
wax or clay image for purposes of revenge. Pins
were stuck into the toad, and as the poor thing
withered and died, the person it represented was expected to do the same. The bones of a toad that had
been used in this cruel way are now in the possession
of a lady in North Wales.

Illustration 1 (Plate XII) shews a clay model of a
human figure, the breast being stuck full of pins. It is
called a "Corp-Chreadh" (clay body or corpse), from
Islay, Scotland, and is preserved in the University
Museum of Archæology and Ethnology at Cambridge.
I    as intended when freshly made to be put in a pool
c    water, and as the clay dissolved, so did the person

c

represented also melt away. The pins must have been put in to make this process as painful as possible.

Other pin superstitions were of a very remarkable character, and when we inform our readers that there were instances of people vomiting pins, we must beg a little patience on their part whilst we explain that this also was considered to be the work of witches, who forced their victims to swallow pins. (How welcome must have been their happy return, as described above, we can well imagine!) Sometimes, however, they were swallowed willingly with the object of wounding the evil spirits of which the swallower believed himself to be possessed. Others are said to have brought up crooked pins without any particular reason, or preparation of any kind, and it was merely thought to be one of the numerous signs of their being bewitched.

Strange to say, there are many instances of people vomiting pins; here is one of the year 1606. "In this year there was a gentlewoman and near kinswoman to Dr. Holland's wife, rector of Exon College, Oxford, strangely bewitched. In her fits she cast out of her nose and mouth pins in great abundance, and did various things very strange to be reported." (From the diary of Walter Young. Camden Society.)

That witches forced their victims to swallow pins is specially stated in an account given in the *Witches of Renfrewshire* (Paisley, 1809) of the bewitching of a young girl named Christian Shaw, daughter of John Shaw of Bargarran, a man of some note in the county. Christian fell into a dead faint, and on recovering, she is said to have "put out of her mouth a great number of pins," which she declared "J. R." had forced into her mouth. Besides pins this young girl is said to have vomited many other things, such as straw, hair, &c., but it appears that from the time when a ball of hair was found in the pocket of one of her tormentors she "put forth" no more. On 10th June 1697, seven witches were burnt for the above-named Christian Shaw.

It would be hard to imagine anything much more disagreeable to swallow than straw and hair, and it is satisfactory to learn that when such things had to be done they were speedily "put forth," to use the elegant expression of that day. It is also a comfort to know that there were antidotes for these strange bewitchments, and at the present time we should very soon pop a ball of hair into the pocket of any one we suspected of being a witch or tormentor of this kind.

An extract from the *Daily Mail* of February 1903 shews that people were then still swallowing pins, but they do not appear to have "put them forth" from "mouth and nose" as neatly as did Miss Christian Shaw of Bargarran. Three doctors were studying the case of the young woman at Naples, and the needles and pins issuing from all parts of her body in a most elaborate manner.

"GIRL SHEDS NEEDLES.—Three doctors are studying the extraordinary case of a young woman, a victim of hysteria, from whose body pins and needles have been issuing for some time past. An examination by means of the Röntgen rays shews that there are still a large number of needles and pins in the young woman's body. The doctors are at a loss to explain the phenomenon, but it is supposed that the girl eats the pins and needles when in an hysterical fit. Admitting this, it is still difficult to explain how they find their way out at her extremities. The girl is said to be a spirit medium and to have made extraordinary revelations when in trances."

The heart is, for obvious reasons, the most remarkable type of charm, and at one time the real heart of a cow, sheep, or cock, in which pins were inserted, was much used in black magic. The following bit of Devonshire folk-lore is interesting as giving an instance of this magic, in some cases called "heart magic"; it also introduces to our notice Mother Sunshine, a white witch, able to counteract the evil influences of black witches.

"'Once upon a time'—in reality about fifty years ago—there existed in a South Devon village two 'Black Witches' named Paddy Goselin and Mary Ann Pyecraft. A certain farmer incurred the anger of Paddy Goselin by pressing for payment of some money he owed. In revenge Paddy Goselin said he would put a spell on the farmer's cattle. Seven bullocks went mad and four died in great agony with their tongues lolling out. (Probably Paddy Goselin gave them yew branches to eat, which would have that effect.) The farmer sent to a white witch in a neighbouring village (named Mother Sunshine). She told him to take the heart of one of the dead bullocks, stick it full of pins and nails and hang it up in the kitchen chimney, and he did so. The still living bullocks quite recovered, and no other cattle suffered. My friend, Mr. Collyer, knew the man who acted for the farmer, and got him to prepare a heart exactly as used by Mother Sunshine." (From a pamphlet by Edward Lovett on *English Charms, Amulets, and Mascots.*)

In Durham there used to be a superstition that

if any one was bewitched, the author of the evil could be discovered by stealing a black cock, out of which the heart was taken and stuck full of pins; if the heart was roasted at "the dead hour of night," the double of the witch would then come and nearly pull the door down. If the double was not seen, any one who had had a remarkably bad night was fixed upon as the culprit. This is indeed a blood-curdling tale, and when we talk of the "dead hour of the night," stealing black cocks and cutting out their hearts, it makes one shudder and cast anxious glances into the dark corners of the room.

No one knows exactly why a black cock should be sacrificed on these occasions, but Lady Wilde in her *Ancient Legends of Ireland* tells us that ancient Egypt and Greece had also superstitions on the subject of sacrificing a cock. And it is worthy of note that a cock bore witness, by his crowing, of St. Peter's treachery.

Lady Wilde also tells us that in some parts of Ireland on St. Patrick's Day a black cock is sacrificed in honour of the saint, though no one can tell why it is considered necessary that blood should be spilt, except that the idea of sacrifice is found in all religions and rituals of worship, and blood must be shed to purify from sin.

A calf's heart stuck full of old wire-headed pins, formerly used as a charm against witchcraft, is preserved in the National Museum of Antiquities in Edinburgh. This is another instance of "heart magic." It was discovered beneath the floor of an old house at Dalkeith, and was presented to the Museum in 1827. (Plate XII., Illustration 2.)

The whole of the district that lies in the imme-

diate neighbourhood of Westminster Abbey is of
great interest, and in Great College Street and some
of the adjoining streets have been found at different
times many proofs of the antiquity of this spot. An
old mill stream formerly wound its way along the
line of Great College Street, and during recent excavations in what was formerly the course of the
stream were discovered a variety of small articles.
Amongst them was a " greybeard " jug corked down,
and when opened it was found to contain a small
piece of cloth or serge, formerly red, of the shape
of a heart, and stuck full of round-headed brass
pins; a small quantity of supposed human hair, and
some clippings of finger-nails. These must once have
constituted a malevolent charm, the intended victim
of which was most likely a woman.

When old buildings are pulled down or excavations made, curious relics are frequently discovered.
In the year 1858 an old cottage in the north of
Scotland was demolished, and in the earth near the
foundations of the walls five or six bottles were found
containing human hair, pins, needles, and fœtid fluid.

In a volume of *Norfolk Annals* published in 1843
we find a curious story about pins in connection with
witchcraft, which seems to have been told to the
Norwich magistrates. A certain Mr. and Mrs Curtis
accused a certain Mrs. Bell of having bewitched them
three days after Tombland Fair, and they had been
bewitched ever since. Mrs. Curtis said she saw
Mrs. Bell light a candle and fill it with pins. She
then proceeded to put some red dragon's blood with
some water into an oyster shell, and, having repeated
a form of words over it, her (Mrs. Curtis's) husband's
arms and legs were set fast, and when he lay down

he could not get up again without help. The man confirmed this statement, and said that Mrs Bell added some parings of her own nails to the dragon's blood and water and put the mixture over the fire, muttering incantations. Poor Mrs. Curtis's husband! history does not relate if he eventually recovered the use of his arms and legs, or if they were for ever "set fast" by Mrs. Bell's bewitchments.

# CHAPTER III

## ROMANTIC SUPERSTITIONS ABOUT PINS — OLD CUSTOMS — PARTICULAR DAYS FAVOURABLE TO THE WORKING OF CHARMS

" Alas! poor Romeo, he is already dead ! stabbed with a white wench's black eye, shot through the ear with a love-song the very pin of his heart cleft with the blind bow-boy's butt-shaft."—*Romeo and Juliet*, Act II. sc. 4.

MANY of the pin superstitions were of a very romantic character, and therefore of particular interest, as there are few lives into which romance has not crept at some time or other.

What it is that really makes the world go round has been a subject of speculation to learned and scientific men in all ages, and we do not pretend to know if they have yet arrived at any satisfactory conclusion. The poets, however, have no hesitation on the subject; they say, " Oh, 'tis love, 'tis love, 'tis love that makes the world go round." This is, anyway, a very charming idea, and people deeply in love are naturally glad to put the feelings of the object of their affections to the test, and would willingly try all kinds of superstitious nonsense to prove to themselves that they not only love, but are loved in return. We have heard of love potions and spells, and the following tale, which is calculated to bring tears to the eyes in more senses than one, may be of use to some of our readers. If a lover did not visit his sweetheart as often as she wished, she roasted

an onion stuck full of ounce pins. The pins must
have never been through paper, and were supposed
to prick his wandering heart and bring him to his
lady's feet. Perhaps an onion was chosen because it
may have been thought to resemble a human heart,
or perhaps because the smell of an onion when cooked
is strong and carries far, and a pathetic message might
in this way be wafted through the air to the lover,
who, his heart thus pricked by the pins, and his nose
tickled by the appetising odour and the pleasures of
anticipation, would more quickly return to his sweetheart.

Particular days and seasons seem to have been
looked upon in all countries as favourable to the
working of charms and superstitious practices. They
are all more or less mixed up with religion, and many
are well known to have descended to us from pagan
times.

In Guernsey the powers of darkness are thought
to be unusually active between Christmas and the
New Year, and it is considered dangerous to be out
after dark; for then, devils, witches, fairies, and
goblins are abroad and active. Perhaps these being
the darkest and longest nights of the year may be
one reason why they are selected for performing spells
by which the secrets of the future may be revealed.
Many other days and nights are also considered
suitable for the working of spells and charms.

The 29th of February, for instance, as it only
comes once in four years, is peculiarly auspicious
to those who desire to have a glance into the future,
especially to young girls burning with anxiety to
know what their husbands will be like. The charm
to be adopted is the following: Twenty-seven of

the smallest pins made must be stuck three by three into a tallow candle; the candle must then be lit up at the wrong end and placed in a candlestick made of clay, which clay must have been taken from a virgin's grave. The candlestick should be placed solemnly upon the left-hand corner of the chimney-piece, exactly as the clock strikes twelve. This must not be done before or after the clock strikes, but during the strokes. The young person working this charm ought now to go to bed, but on no account to sleep, for the candle must be watched, and when it has quite burnt out, the pins must be put into the left shoe. All being ready sleep may now be sought, and before nine nights have passed away fate will reveal itself.

For St John's Eve (June 23rd) a new pincushion of the very best black velvet (no inferior quality will do) is necessary. On one side the name of the person concerned must be stuck in full length with the smallest pins procurable (none other will do). On the other side a cross must be made with very large pins surrounded by a circle, also of pins. Place the pincushion in a stocking taken off at night, and still warm from contact with its owner's foot. The stocking should then be hung at the foot of the bed, and if these directions have been carefully followed, the future life of the owner of the pincushion and the stocking will pass before her during the night in a dream.

These are very elaborate programmes, and it would be difficult to carry them out to the letter; but doubtless the end to be obtained is worth much trouble. St. John the Baptist is usually represented with a long wand in his hand surmounted by a cross;

this may give a reason for the cross put up on the black velvet pincushion. St. John's Eve is also kept as a holiday and fête in most Christian lands, it is therefore naturally thought to be a favourable night for inviting dreams.

St. Agnes' Eve (January 20th) was formerly a night of great importance to young women who wished to know whom they would marry. "St. Agnes, virgin and martyr, A D. 304, suffered martyrdom so young and with such fortitude, that the tongues and pens of all nations "—says St. Jerome—"are employed to celebrate her praise. Her legend (one of the earliest in the Christian Church) says she refused to become the wife of the son of the Roman Prefect, having devoted herself to the service of God, and he, in revenge, denounced her as a Christian. Upon her refusal to sacrifice to the gods, she was brutally tortured and stripped, and angels immediately veiled her whole person with her hair. Her persecutors then lighted a large pile of faggots, and threw her into the midst; and the flames were at once extinguished without at all injuring her. She was then beheaded. Some time after her death, while her parents were praying by her grave, she appeared to them with a glorified aspect and a white lamb by her side, and bade them dry their tears, for she was united for ever to her Saviour in Heaven." (From *The Calendar of the Anglican Church* )

No doubt the beautiful life of this youthful martyr, her fortitude under torture and devotion in death, have kept the memory of St. Agnes green, and St. Agnes' Eve for ever consecrated to young maidens and their dreams of love and marriage.

The following is a good receipt to be used on

this night by young men and women who wish to catch a glimpse of their future wives or husbands. A row of pins is taken, and whilst each pin is being pulled out separately, a paternoster must be said. Then, if one pin is stuck into the sleeve, the future will be revealed in a dream. This is a very simple mode of settling a most momentous question.

There seem to be many ingenious ways of doing this, and in some places they take the blade-bone of a rabbit, stick nine pins in it, and then put it under their pillows, and during the night they are sure to see the object of their affections.

Twelfth-Night was at one time thought auspicious, not only for dreams, but for revels of rather a peculiar and amusing description. On this night boys assembled round pastry-cooks' shops, where tempting goods displayed in the windows attracted passers-by to linger. They used quickly and dexterously to nail the coat-tails of those people who ventured near enough, to the bottom of the window frames, or pin them together strongly by their clothes  Sometimes eight or ten persons would find themselves thus pinned together, and in order to escape they must either leave part of their coat behind them, or go off with a hole in it. Shouts of laughter from the perpetrators and spectators filled the air, and it often happened that the one who laughed most at the detention of another, would turn round and find himself also unable to move. All efforts to gain freedom increased the mirth, nor was the presence of a policeman able to stop the mischief.

This must indeed have been a cheery game, to put it mildly, and one can easily imagine it would have been hard work for even a large party of policemen to put a stop to so wild a scene when the revels were at their height.

St. Thomas' Eve is another favourite night for the working of love spells and charms, and in *Guernsey Folk-Lore*, edited by Miss Edith Carey, we learn that on this night girls who wish to know whom they will marry must go through several mysterious rites when retiring to bed. They must first of all secure a golden pippin and pass two pins crossways through it, and then lay it down under their pillow. Opinions differ as to the exact way in which this ritual should be performed. It is thought best by some to wrap the pippin up in the stocking taken from the left leg ; others take this stocking off last, and throw it over the left shoulder. We do not know which is right, but there seems to be no doubt as to what follows. It is *absolutely* necessary to get into bed backwards. All that has gone before is useless if the bed is reached in any other way, and the following incantation must then be repeated three times :—

> "Saint Thomas, Saint Thomas,
> Le plus court, le plus bas,
> Fais moi voir en m'endormant
> Celui qui sera mon amant,
> Et le pays, et le contrée
> Où il fait sa demeurée,
> Et le métier qu'il sait faire
> Devant moi qu'il vienne faire
> Qu'il soit beau ou qu'il soit laid.
> Tel qu'il sera je l'aimerai
> Saint Thomas, fait moi la grâce
> Que je le vois, que je l'embrasse
> Ainsi soit il."

Not another word must be spoken, and, if the rite has been duly performed, the desired knowledge will be communicated in a dream.

Another charm consists in placing fronds of agrimony, each bearing nine leaflets, crosswise under the pillow, and securing them by two new pins, also crossed. The future husband will then appear in a dream.

Children in Guernsey do not forget the 1st April. They use crooked pins to fasten long shreds of paper or bits of rag to the clothes of passers-by, and then cry out as loud as they can bawl, "La Coûe! La Coûe!" or "La folle Agnes." No one knows the reason of the last exclamation.

These islanders also tell us how to remove a spell and cause the person who cast it to appear. This knowledge may be useful, though the preparations are certainly gruesome. But, if a spell has to be removed, the superstitious, though they may be very tender-hearted, will stick at nothing. In this case, alas! a pigeon must be killed, and its heart plucked out. The heart must be stuck all round with new pins, and then thrown into a pot of boiling water. A piece of green turf is used as a cover to the pot, and must be put on with the earth downwards. A good fire of wood or charcoal must be carefully kept up, and at the end of an hour the heart is thrown into the burning embers. If all the doors and windows are carefully closed, the sorcerer will come and call, or knock at the door, but it must on no account be opened until he has promised to remove the spell.

On St. Thomas' Eve in Derbyshire girls used to procure a large red onion, into which, after it was peeled, they stuck nine pins, and said :—

> "Good St. Thomas, do me right,
> Send me my true love this night,
> In his clothes and his array
> Which he weareth every day."

One pin was placed in the centre, and the other eight stuck round it. The centre one was given the name of the "true love." The onion thus prepared was placed under the pillow on going to bed, and the girl dreamt of the right person.

There is a curious superstition connected with the Chapel of St. Aldhelm (built in the twelfth century), St Aldhelm's Head, Dorsetshire, one of the oldest and smallest churches in England. It is only about thirty feet square, and the vaulted stone roof, low and slightly pyramidal, is supported by arches which spring from a central pillar. There is a superstition connected with the pillar to the effect that if a pin is put in a certain hole while a wish is mentally registered, the wish will be fulfilled. We are told tradition connects the practice with a wish "for a husband," and that possibly young girls still put their pins into the hole and wish.

Indo-Mohammedan folk-lore provides us with a charming story of an enchantment worked with pins.

A sorceress having fallen deeply in love with a fascinating prince, is naturally much injured on finding her advances rejected, and plans revenge. She determines to surprise the prince on coming from the bath; and having provided herself with a bag, which she takes from her girdle at the right moment and blows upon, a shower of pins fly from it and pierce the prince in every part of his body, till he falls insensible. Many years afterwards a princess having lost her way in the jungle, suddenly comes upon a ruined city and palace. She enters the palace, and there, extended on a couch, lies the prince, his body full of pins. She pulls them all out, thus destroying the spell; and the prince, restored to health and vigour, being more fascinating than ever, imagination supplies the sequel.

This is a delightful specimen of the pin superstitions from, perhaps, the most romantic part of the whole British Empire. They existed in great variety in all parts of the world; some still exist; and in Russia, to this day, it is an omen of evil to meet a priest on leaving a house, which can be charmed away only by throwing a pin at him if you are a woman, and by spitting on his beard if you are a man. This is rather unpleasant, but in Iceland a much more revolting superstition was practised. If there was any fear that a man would walk after his death, pins and needles were thrust into the feet of the corpse; but to drive a nail into a dead man's tomb in the interval that passes between the reading of the epistle and the gospel, was a less offensive remedy and seems to have been thought equally efficacious.

We still sometimes think it necessary to give a small piece of money in return for the present of a knife or a pair of scissors, as they are otherwise considered unlucky presents to receive. Some trifle given in return is thought to break the spell. This superstition existed with the rest in days gone by, and it was thought then, as it is now, unlucky to give a knife, a pair of scissors, or any sharp instrument to a person one loved, as these things would cut love and friendship. If a pin or a farthing were given in return the ill effects might be eluded. Lord Byron is said to have given Lady Blessington a pin which he frequently wore in his breast, for a keepsake. But he afterwards begged her to accept a chain instead, "as memorials with a point are of less fortunate augury."

In some countries a charm is used by one un-married person to compel the love of another, "to turn the heart" of the indifferent; but the sad story of Ben Hudson and his wife shews that a charm was also used to regain a husband's love. At Derby, on 15th July 1873, Benjamin Hudson was found guilty of having murdered his wife, and was condemned to be hanged. In the pocket of the murdered woman was found a purse containing some pins and a piece of paper, on which the deceased had written :—

> "It's not the pins I mean to burn,
> But Ben Hudson's heart I mean to turn;
> Let him neither eat, speak, drink, nor comfort find,
> Till he comes to me and speaks his mind."

The husband was twenty-four and the wife twenty-three. They seem to have cared for each other in spite of their quarrels and jealousies, and the charm, no doubt, was to regain her husband's love.

About seventy years ago a curious custom prevailed at Grantham. Girls used to go and peep into the crypt belonging to Grantham Church (at that time full of bones, which were still there in 1857, but have now been cleared away, and the crypt used for the heating apparatus of the church), and every time they did so they threw in a pin, to prevent bad luck, or perhaps as a kind of "douceur" to the ghosts which might be supposed to hang about the place; in consideration of which they were expected to refrain from haunting the person who had thus "remembered" them. Money would have been thrown away in such a cause, and so a metallic object which scarcely any one would fail to be able to give may have been taken as its symbol, and no doubt it passed for money's worth in the shades below!

D

Young people, like fools, rush in "where angels fear to tread," and one can well imagine the timorous joy of peeping into this gloomy abode, the doing of which they no doubt believed would lead to endless misfortune, but for the pins thrown in with fervent faith.

An old lady who died in the early part of the last century thought it unlucky to meet a funeral; so whenever she went out driving, took a store of pins in her carriage, and was happy in the belief that if on meeting a funeral she threw plenty of pins out of the carriage window, this would avert any ill-luck the encounter might otherwise have caused.

It would, no doubt, be a great relief to many superstitious people now if, when obliged to pass under a ladder, or when caught unawares by a new moon on looking out of a closed window without having first consulted an almanack, they could throw pins about and thus disperse the ill effects of such unfortunate circumstances.

A volume of *Curious Articles from the "Gentleman's Magazine,"* published in 1809, furnishes some interesting details concerning the swallowing of pins and fish-bones, which may be useful, as this custom, though not romantic, is still in fashion, and has often been the cause of very dangerous, and sometimes fatal, results; for, upon dissecting patients, it has been found they have been killed by pins. In April 1777, a young woman who had swallowed a very large pin which stuck fast in her throat was taken to the hospital at Bamborough Castle, Northumberland. The doctor who then had the principal management of that hospital was sent for, and found the patient in great pain. Having some time before studied the nature of these accidents, he immediately gave her four grains of tartar emetic dissolved in warm water, and then made her swallow the white of six eggs, and in about three minutes it all returned *with the pin*, and she was effectually relieved. The same treatment was successful in an instance nearly resembling the above. It seems hardly credible, but a maid-servant to the Honourable Mrs. Baillie of Mellerstain, in Scotland, went to bed with twenty-four pins in her mouth. The consequence was that in the night the family were alarmed by her screams. Mr. Baillie ordered her an emetic and the whites of eggs, as above; the whole number of pins reappeared, and, we are told, are preserved in the family as curiosities.

We will now turn to pleasanter subjects, and speak of our sailors, who, though the bravest of men and the most romantic, are proverbially superstitious, and pay great attention to anything that bears in the smallest degree upon the subject. Amongst other things, they used to believe that pins were spiteful witches and should never be brought on board ship, as they would bring more ill with them than the opening of Pandora's box itself.

There is a great sameness of diet on board a smack, but the quantity consumed is prodigious. It is sometimes a little varied by exchanges with passing vessels and occasional parcels by the carrier boat. In order to shew how great was the superstitious fear of pins amongst sailors, we relate the tale of a parcel sent on board a vessel wrapped in a clean white napkin fastened with pins. The parcel contained a large apple tart. It was clear something was amiss directly it was handed on board. One man held the parcel; the captain cautiously took out each pin, and, with

arm extended to the uttermost, carefully dropped
them over into the sea to drown, the whole ceremony
being gone through separately with each pin.    The
captain then seriously and solemnly assured every
one present that pins were spiteful witches and ought
never to be brought on board a vessel.    He afterwards
declared that to these pins he owed a leak necessitating
pump-work every half-hour; a more than usually
large number of holes in their nets; and, finally, the
loss of all their gear in a heavy sea which compelled
them to return immediately to port.

# CHAPTER IV

## PIN HILL AND PIN WELLS

" Flow on, then, for ever, thou clear crystal rill,
Flow on, then, exhaustless, from out of the hill,
May beauty oft seek thee to muse on the spell
That clings to the pins as they sink in the well "

IN those good old days when there were dragons,
seven-headed serpents, wizards, giants, and all kinds
of delightful people that charm the hearts of children,
there were also many other wonderful and fabulous
things; we have even heard of a glass mountain,
at the top of which lived a beautiful princess who
would only accept as a husband he who could scale
the slippery heights of glass and claim her hand
in person! But who ever heard of Pin Hill—a hill
of pins? Once upon a time, however, about seventy
years ago, there was a place on the west side of Hard-
wicke Hill, in the parish of Scotton, Lincolnshire,
called Pin Hill, and though not high enough to climb,
it was none the less strange on that account; for at
this spot a mound about the size of a heap of gravel
lay by the roadside, composed of pins and broken
tobacco pipes. The pins were not brittle, nor were
they in any way different from common pins. The
story in the neighbourhood was, that a ship laden with
pins had been wrecked there. Why these things were
deposited on Scotton Common it is impossible to
say, but there must have been some good magical
reason for it. We have ascertained from a resident
in that neighbourhood, that Pin Hill is only three-

quarters of a mile from the river Trent, which at this
point is tidal, and sea-going vessels can, and do, come
up at high tide.   The intervening ground between
Pin Hill and the river is flat, some of it at any rate
*below* the level of the river, so that before the banking
of the Trent by the Dutch (supposed to have taken
place during the reign of Charles II.) it would have
been quite possible for a small vessel to have been
wrecked, or to have run aground there.   Pin Hill is
quite thirty miles from the sea, and is still known
by that name, though our correspondent from the
neighbourhood has never heard of the mound of pins,
nor has he smoked any of the tobacco pipes !

There must, of course, have been some good foundation for this story, but we can find no more pin
hills !   There were, however, amongst the Holy wells
with which the world is scattered, a great number
that in Great Britain especially were called Pin wells ;
many still exist, and there is no superstition stronger
than a belief in the curative powers of their waters.
Travellers have described the votive offerings left
upon the trees that shadow the sacred walls of Persia,
Egypt, and other distant lands ; they were tokens of
gratitude to the patron saint of the well, for health
restored  or  blessings  received  at  them.   The  pins
thrown in were to propitiate the saints to whom the
wells were dedicated, and represented the more precious offerings of olden days.   These offerings probably originated in the pagan worship of water (water
being one of the greatest blessings), though through
the lapse of ages they have lost some of their original
significance, and are now practised more as ancient
customs, which, having come down to us through
many generations, are naturally looked upon with great

reverence. A well is a magnet to which all are drawn in every land, be it desert or city, and much that is beautiful has been written about them. At the Well of Wisdom under the protection of the god Mimir, Odin by drinking thereof became the wisest of all beings. "Truth is said to lie at the bottom of a well, and surely beauty is always found at its surface. Here earth bares her breasts to all her children, and trees, and beasts, and men alike drink of her strength. In our childhood's stories what significance lay in the name of a well! In the sweetest fairy-tales how often has imagination drunk its fill at the Magic Well! And in the Book of Life itself history has paused at the well-side to tell some of her most beautiful stories." This passage, from the late Lieutenant Boyd Alexander's book, *From the Niger to the Nile*, shews we are not receding from the regions of romance when we take up the subject of wells, but rather advancing into the very heart of that mysterious land; though the wells we shall shortly refer to are not like those he describes, " in a country of fierce heat," but are situated in different parts of the British Isles, and from time to time beyond the memory of man have been held to cure diseases. One well is reputed to be good for sprains, another is good for sore eyes, another enables the deaf to hear, and yet another cures nervous diseases. No doubt in very ancient times it was enough to wash the lame leg or bathe the sore eyes with the water of these Holy wells, having perfect faith in their power to cure; but, later, offerings were made. "The custom of throwing pins into sacred wells, and of tying rags to bushes, especially to bushes growing near to sacred wells, has exercised students in folk-lore ever since folk-lore came to be studied. They seem such odd practices that—until one has learnt that most human practices, however odd and senseless they may appear, have their reasons and are not mere caprices—it is not easy to suppose they ever had a reasonable basis. When one knows there is a hidden meaning, the question 'What is that meaning?' has been a very perplexing one. If a suggestion is offered it is hardly in the hope of settling the matter so much as of drawing attention to a habit of archaic thought running through many a habit of archaic practice, and possibly therefore affecting the customs. In the customs at wells, trees, and temples we have another application of the same reasoning as that which underlies the practices of witchcraft. If an article of my clothing in a witch's hands may make me suffer, the same article in contact with a beneficial person will relieve my pain and restore me to health and wealth. A pin that pricked my wart, has by its contact acquired a peculiar bond with the wart, so that whatever is done to the pin, the same is brought to bear upon the wart. If my name is written upon the walls of a temple, or a stone from my hand cast upon a sacred image, it is henceforth in continual contact with divinity. When a girl pupil of the Ursuline nuns of Quintin marries and enters an interesting situation, the nuns send her a white silk ribbon painted in blue (virgin colours) with the words 'Notre-Dame de délivrance protégez-vous.' Before sending it off they touch with it the Reliquary of the parish church, which contains a fragment of the Virgin's Zone. The recipient hastens to fasten the ribbon around her waist, and does not cease to wear it till her baby is born. For the ribbon having

been in contact with the divinity, though the contact
has outwardly ceased, is still in some subtle connection
with the goddess." (From an article in *Folk-lore*,
by Sidney Hartland (1893), vol. iv. p. 451.)

The object of visiting Holy wells was, as has
already been said, mainly for the cure of diseases.
The usual ritual was to walk round the wells one or
more times sun-ways, to drink the water, to wet a
fragment of their clothing with it, and to attach this
fragment to any tree or bush that happened to be
near the wells. This fragment having been in contact
with the water from the Holy well, was supposed to
relieve the pain and restore the health of the person
to whom it belonged, in the same way that the
ribbon sent by the Ursuline nuns of Quintin, which
had touched the Reliquary of the church, was thought
to protect and restore the health of their pupil. The
rags or fragments of clothing were "vehicles of the
diseases," the pins were the offerings; and after
repeating a prayer in which they mentioned their ail-
ments, the ceremony was ended by dropping in a pin.
The wells were also visited for acquiring charms for
protection against witches and fairies, and generally
the securing of good luck. But when visited for
these purposes the rags were dispensed with. We
have said that the rags were "the vehicles of the
diseases," but we believe they were also offerings in
some places, and Miss Eleanor Alexander especially
mentions this in *Lady Anne's Walk*. She says: "Pins
are in many ways preferable for obvious reasons; but
there is a certain pathos in the votive offerings of
pitiful, dirty little uneven patches of discoloured
stuffs, which may be stuck on the thorns of hedge
or bush beside a Holy well."

We must now draw attention to Plate XIII., Illustration 1, which represents a young woman in the act of dropping a pin into a well at Barenton in Brittany; and we are told in *Folk-lore of Scottish Lochs and Springs*, by J. M. Mackinlay, that should good fortune await those who drop pins into this well, the water will send up bubbles. If it remains quite still, no good luck can be expected. Many people may like to know the reputed powers of the different waters to be found in the Pin wells of Great Britain and Ireland; we will therefore now describe some of the principal ones, and explain where they are to be found.

Beginning with England, we will go first to Cornwall, for it is said that pins were collected in handfuls near Holy wells in that county, and the custom is still kept up at many of them. The famous well dedicated to St Madron was a very popular resort for those who sought relief from aches and pains, and St. Madron was always propitiated by an offering of pins or pebbles. He is honoured at a church near the Land's End, and close by is the well. Mr. J. M. Mackinlay tells us St. Madron's Well was visited on May morning by maidens wishing to discover their matrimonial fate. They took two pieces of straw, about an inch in length, and placing them crossways, fastened them together with a pin. The cross was then thrown into the spring, and the rising bubbles carefully counted, for they corresponded with the years which would pass before the arrival of the wedding-day.

One of the characters in Sir Walter Scott's *Pirate* expresses a wish that providence would send a wreck to gladden the hearts of the Shetlanders. At the other extremity of Britain, viz. in the Scilly Islands,

PLATE XIII

1. Fontaine Ste. Barbe (Wishing Well) at Barenton, Brittany.

2. St. Mary's Wishing Well, Orton, Morayshire.

3. St. George's Wishing Well, in the Parish of Ste. Marie du Castel, Guernsey.

the same hope was at one time cherished. St. Warna, who was thought to preside over shipwrecks, was the patron saint of St. Agnes, one of the islands of the group. She had her Holy well, and there the natives formerly dropped in a crooked pin and called upon the saint to send them a rich wreck. At St. Nun's Well, close to Pelynt (Cornwall), a great number of pins were thrown in, not only by those who visited it out of curiosity, but also by those who wished to avail themselves of the virtue of its waters. It is thought to be efficacious for the cure of insanity. A well near St. Austell, at Menacuddle, received crooked pins as offerings, and it was believed that the pins which had been thrown in by former devotees would be seen to rise from their beds to greet the new-comer before it touched the bottom. The Holy well at Roche is frequented by the peasantry before sunrise on Holy Thursday and the two following Thursdays. Offerings of pins are made to the guardian saint; sometimes they are bent before being thrown in.

St. Keyne has bequeathed to a well in Cornwall, and also to one in South Wales, the power of bestowing the mastery on whichever of a young couple first drinks of it after their marriage. One aggrieved husband confesses his wife's superior wisdom in these lines :—

> " I hastened as soon as the wedding was done,
> And left my wife in the porch,
> But i' faith, she had been wiser than me,
> For she took a bottle to church ! "
>
> —SOUTHEY

Those who do not wish to travel so far as Cornwall in search of a Pin well can go to Chepstow in Monmouth-shire, where they will find one which, though it has not the interesting properties of St. Keyne's, is still in some repute for its healing powers. It is also a wishing well, and a lady of our acquaintance dropped a pin into it and wished her wish, only a year ago. Whether the wish has been fulfilled we know not, such things being usually kept a profound secret.

Those who visit the Isle of Wight will find two wells inside Carisbrook Castle · one in present use inside the well-house, and the other up in the keep. The latter is now filled up with rubbish, and quite unfit for use. When the one in present use was cleaned out some years ago, a quantity of pins were found. We are told in Timbs' *Abbeys, Castles, and Ancient Halls* that both these wells were at one time famed for having the property of echoing the fall of a pin in a most singular manner. A lady now residing at Carisbrook Castle informs us that this is still the case, and that the well now used is so beautifully constructed that the slightest echo can easily be heard. The fall of a drop of water is quite distinct, but visitors are now requested to refrain from throwing down any article which might render the water impure. When the pins were found in this well, a great many pence were also discovered, and one Charles I. shilling.

There was once a Pin well near the railway station at Lewes in Sussex. It seems to have disappeared, but there is a street called Pin Street close to where the well used to be. This shews its memory is kept green by the inhabitants of Lewes, and that the pins, like "Truth," did lie at the bottom of *that* well.

Travelling into the Eastern Counties we come to the celebrated wells at Walsingham in Norfolk. In the Priory of Our Lady of Walsingham are two wells and a bath, and from time immemorial they have all three been designated as "Wishing Wells," and were believed to cure headaches and indigestion. No doubt offerings were made, and pins dropped into them at some time or other, though the custom seems now to have been forgotten.

Going further north, we find St. Helen's Well at Sephton in Lancashire was used as a Pin well until eleven or twelve years ago. The well was till then an open one, and it supplied the neighbourhood with water for drinking purposes. But there were so many well-founded complaints that tramps used it for their ablutions and passers-by washed their dogs in it, that it received a lid of stout planking, and was after a time boarded up, so that all access to the water is now prevented. It is shut off from the road by an iron railing, outside which a pump is fixed; the flow of water is still abundant, but of course all romantic associations are destroyed. The pin-dropping continued in full force until the well was covered up, and it was cleaned out twice yearly, when pins were removed. The supposition was that if the point of the pin settled on the bottom directed towards the church, the person who dropped it would be married within the year: how the notion arose it is difficult to say. The pin-dropping did not die out, but was simply made impossible.

Near to Wooler in Northumberland, beautifully situated in a valley on the flanks of the Cheviots, there is a very famous Pin well at which, on May Day, the most charming customs have been long observed.

It is variously called the Fairy, Wishing, Maiden, or Pin well, and on May Day morning a crowd of people anxious to conciliate its presiding spirit, used to form a procession, which, wending its way from the town into Glendale, where lies the well, there made a stop ; each person in the procession dropped a crooked pin into the water, at the same time wishing a wish, in the honest belief that the spirit of the well would, before the New Year came, fulfil this wish. The procession no longer takes place on May Day, but the superstitions connected with it have not entirely disappeared. Young people still repair to the well and drop in their pins, whispering the name of their lovers with the same ardent zeal. The number of crooked pins always to be seen at the bottom of the well prove that this custom is still kept up, and even old people pause before questioning the virtue of the ceremony.

A local poet, in singing the praises of the well, also describes the uses to which it is now put, in the following verses :—

" Deep down in a vale 'midst the hills of my birth
There springs a clear fountain, the purest on earth,
Through the wide world no nectar can ever excel
The water that flows from our wishing Pin well.

Flow on, then, for ever, thou clear crystal rill,
Flow on, then, exhaustless, from out of the hill,
May beauty oft seek thee to muse on the spell
That clings to the pins as they sink in the well.

There, oft in my boyhood, in sunny midday,
I've laved my hot forehead, all throbbing with play ;
What scenes of wild gladness my memory could tell,
As I sported and ran round the rocks by the well
Flow on, then, &c

There, oft in the gloaming, with everything still
Save the blackbird's soft melody poured o'er the hill
I've dreamt it was Eden, that wild craggy dell,
While I knelt with my Eve on the brink of the well.
Flow on, then, &c.

The wishers that bent them, far scattered may roam
Away from that spring 'mid the hills of their home,
But what wishes remain, who their number can tell,
That still hover, unseen, round their pins in the well?
Flow on, then, &c.

Should fortune e'er lead me afar o'er the sea,
And tear me from scenes I love dearly, and thee,
Neither absence, nor distance, can ever dispel
The charm of these scenes round that magical well
Flow on, then, &c."

Imagination conjures up the scenes described in this pretty poem; and as nothing seems so far to have occurred to prevent the dropping in of pins, those who happen to be in the neighbourhood, or do not mind a seven or eight hours' journey from London, with several changes, can find their way to this fairy well, wish their wishes, and drop in as many pins as they like—there seems to be no restriction!

Let us now make our way into Wales, that home of poetry and legend, where, the silent solitude of its mountains having made the Welshman both imaginative and impressionable, the legends and super-stitions of its Holy wells find in him the most ardent of believers. The pin-dropping was a well-known custom both in North and South Wales. The pin was usually a crooked one, and this may be ex-plained upon the supposed hypothesis in folk-lore, that crooked things are lucky things, as a crooked sixpence, &c.

The most famous of Welsh wells is undoubtedly St. Winnefred's at Holywell in Flintshire. It is considered miraculous for the cure of many com-plaints, and the walls which surround the spring are hung with crutches and other offerings left by grateful pilgrims. No doubt the pin has also been offered here, for in several accounts of this well we read that " the water is so clear, a pin could be plainly seen lying at the bottom of it." Near to this celebrated well is a small spring, once famed for the cure of weak eyes. The patient made an offering of a crooked pin to the nymph of the spring, and sent up at the same time a prayer by way of charm. But the charm is forgotten, and the power of the waters lost.

The spring known as Holy Well, or Cefyn Bryn (a mountain in Glamorganshire), was much resorted to for the cure of sore eyes, and the pins dropped into it seem to have had the same power of welcoming new-comers as those in the well near Saint Austell in Cornwall. This one was supposed to be under the special patronage of the Virgin Mary, and a crooked pin was the offering of every visitor. It was believed that if a pin was dropped in with fervent faith, all the pins already there might be seen rising from the bottom to greet the new one! Argue the impossibility of the thing, and you are told that it is true it never happens *now*, such earnestness of faith being, alas! no more.

The well still exists, but is no longer visited for the sake of benefits to be derived from drinking its water. The custom was much in vogue about sixty years ago, and the present incumbent of a parish near by remembers, when a child, being often taken to drink the water and drop in a pin. It was quite a small, open pool, with a strong spring of water running through it. There was no fence round it of any kind. It is situated on the north side of Cefyn Bryn, under High Hill. Bits of rag were also seen tied to small twigs and stuck round the edge of this spring.

There is a subterranean well under the ruins of Carreg Cennen Castle, in the parish of Llandilo in Carmarthenshire, into which pins are even now dropped to procure the speedy realisation of wishes. So we see that Wales does not differ from England in having the same traditions and superstitions attached to its wells and springs.

Should we now feel inclined to make our way to Holyhead, and cross over to that Emerald Isle which Dean Hole has called " the beautiful land of the merry-hearted," we shall there find the same Holy wells and the same superstitious belief in the curative powers of their waters. The ritual is much the same at all these places of pilgrimage. The pilgrims go round the well either three or nine times on all fours. They must, as elsewhere, go from east to west, following the course of the sun and repeating paters and aves the whole time. After each round they make a small heap of stones, and the one who has the most heaps, having said the most prayers, will receive the greatest honour in Paradise. These wells are usually reached by going down some steps ; and the patient, kneeling beside it, bathes his forehead and hands in the water. The disease or pain from which he suffers will then gradually leave him. Whenever a white thorn or an ash tree grows near a well, that well is considered exceptionally sacred, and the patient having drunk of the water, before leaving the spot ties a votive offering to a branch of the tree. This may be a coloured handkerchief, or a red strip taken from a garment. Lady Wilde tells us in *Ancient Legends of Ireland* that " these offerings are never

E

removed, they remain for years fluttering in the wind and the rain." Numerous offerings of pins and pebbles are also made.

At the foot of Knocklade, a mountain near Cape Castle, Co. Antrim, is a Holy well called "The Well of the Eye," the waters of which are good for sore eyes. If the water is used for bathing them on the spot or taken away in a bottle, some offering is left in return. At one time this used to be a pebble dropped upon a certain cairn, but later a pin was placed in a certain hole in a stone, where quite recently they have been seen by visitors.

We presume that the "Well of the Eye" was dedicated to Saint Bridget, to whom all wells efficacious in the cure of sore eyes are dedicated. Miss Eleanor Alexander in *Lady Anne's Walk* relates the tradition that "Bridget had early dedicated herself to the service of God, and the life of a nun. But she was a very taking girl, with remarkably fine eyes, and several excellent parties, backed up, of course, by her relations, tried to induce her to change her mind. There was one gentleman in especial who would take no refusal. When she was walking with him one day he paid her an early Irish compliment on her beautiful eyes. She looked away to hide her blushes, and when she turned to him again, the amorous chieftain perceived with dismay that she had plucked out one of her eyes, and that it was hanging down her cheek. As she was a saint, she did not, of course, wink with the other when he precipitately withdrew all pretensions to her hand. As soon as he had gone, she bathed her face in a well close by, and her eye was at once restored to its proper position, and was as good as ever."

In the neighbourhood of Armagh there are several Pin wells, and all who seek a cure at them drop a pin into the water. Bushels of pins were also lately cleared out of a Holy well near Newry.

Another well in Westmeath, at Crooked Wood, near Mullingar, is supposed to cure all diseases, and we know for a fact that pins are thrown in to this day.

People are frequently seen kneeling beside the Holy wells in Donegal, and the trees and bushes near by are covered with bits of rag One well near Letterkenny is very famous as a cure for every kind of disease; sticks, crutches, and rags surround it, and though we are not able to gather any positive information with regard to pins, it is most likely they were used as offerings also, at some time or other.

On the coast of County Galway, near to Cleggan, are two wells. One is dedicated to Saint Gregory, and is said to have sprung up on the spot where he dropped his own head! The legend being that his head was cut off, and that he afterwards walked three hundred yards carrying it under his arm! At the other well ten virgins are supposed to have been drowned. Pins are dropped into both wells even now, and if, on visiting them, the sun shines on those already there, it is thought a good omen for the visitor. From Cleggan there is a fine view of a beautiful range of mountains, called the "Twelve Pins," on account of their twelve pointed heads. The highest is 2895 feet, and one is named the "Diamond Pin." Dean Hole gives an amusing account of his visit to this neighbourhood, and of his first view of the "Twelve Pins." He was driving in some public conveyance, and describes a "party from Sheffield"

seated on the box, who had no sooner ascertained from
the driver that the grand highlands before him were
known as the "Twelve Pins," than he desired the
company to inform him "what degree of relationship
existed between them and the Needles off the Isle of
Wight." He then asked the company a riddle, "Why
have them pins no pints? Because they're principally
quartz!" The Dean also describes his visit to a Holy
well in County Cork, situated upon an island called
Gougane-barra on Lake Allua, of which the Irish
poet Callanan sings ·—

> "There is a green island on lone Gougane-barra
> Where Allua of songs rushes forth as an arrow."

The Dean says he reached the "green island" by an
overland route, a method of access which he does not
remember to have noticed out of Ireland!

Many wonderful cures have been performed at
the Holy well on this island, and it is still visited by
pilgrims. Some steps lead down to the well, and
there is a little ledge round the inside of it, where
pins in all stages of rust and decay can be seen, besides
bright new ones. A party of tourists was there
quite recently and saw the pins in great numbers.

And now, before saying farewell to the Emerald Isle,
we must relate an interesting little story about a pin,
told us by a gentleman who visited County Galway
in the summer of 1901. He was staying in a small
village, and had made great friends with an old miller
belonging to the place. This old man took him for
walks in the neighbourhood every day. One morning
they started as usual, and were passing along a very
picturesque pathway, when suddenly the old man
stopped and turned back, saying, "We must not go

that way to-day." On being asked an explanation for so suddenly changing his mind, he pointed to a crooked pin lying on the path and said, " Nothing will ever make me take any path that has *that* lying in my way!" So they turned and went back to the mill. This seems a singular contradiction of the belief that, generally speaking, crooked pins are lucky ones. But perhaps, in Ireland anyway, the idea is that bad luck is. thrown away with a crooked pin, and remains with the pin wherever it lies (as is thought to be the case with the rags at the wells), so that in walking over or picking up a crooked pin, the bad luck thrown away with it may be picked up or passed on also. But, as an old Scotchman once said, " We maun keep the customs of our fathers," and we have heard that " men do more things from custom than from reason"; so, as custom seems stronger than reason, and is also said to be "a second nature," there seems no use in arguing the matter further. We will therefore continue our imaginary journey, and leaving Ireland, with its many-coloured rags fluttering in the breeze round her wells, and the sun shining on the pins within them, take a peep at the Isle of Man on our way to Scotland.

This island was early conquered by the Northmen or warriors of Scandinavia, and the Manxman inherits from them traditions and legends of sea-kings and pirates. Sir Walter Scott says of this island in *Peveril of the Peak:* " Superstition, too, had her tales of fairies, ghosts, and spectres—her legends of saints and demons, of fairies and familiar spirits, which in no corner of the British Empire are told or received with more absolute credulity than in the Isle of Man." It is therefore with fresh zeal and ever-increasing

interest that we land on this island and find our way
to its most celebrated well, which is dedicated to
Saint Maughold, one of the earliest Manx saints.

Saint Maughold's Well had its full virtue only
when visited on the first Sunday of harvest. There
is evidence that within the last ten years, if not at the
present time, the water of this well was considered
to be also especially efficacious for the cure of sore
eyes. Professor Rhys was told that when it was applied
for this purpose, it was customary, after using it on
the spot or filling a bottle with it to take home,
to drop a pin, a bead, or a button into the well.

From information gathered through the kindness
of friends in the island, it seems that the pin-dropping
is done now chiefly by visitors, who, having heard of
the old custom, look upon it as a wishing-well and
drop in their pins for luck.

In Baldwin, a valley near Douglas, there is a well
called "Chibber Uner." Chibber means "well," and
Uner is a corruption of Chibber Runer, Runius
being the patron saint of Marown, in which parish is
the well. Pins are still dropped into it. At another
well in Man, called Chibber Undin (Foundation
Well), in the parish of Malew, the patient used to walk
twice round the well with water from it in his mouth;
he finally emptied that water into a piece of stuff torn
from any garment he might be wearing; this fragment
was tied to the branch of a hawthorn tree which grew
there, and left to rot away; the disease supposed to
cling to it then died also. It was thought that any
one rash enough to take away a rag thus deposited,
would be sure to contract the disease communicated to
it by the person who left it there. Walking round
the well was the ritual observed in connection with

all the sacred wells in Man, but Chibber Undin is the only one where it is necessary to hold the water in the mouth whilst doing so.

There are many places of great historical interest in the Isle of Man besides the wells, and fain would we linger amongst them; but this being impossible, let us pass on and imagine ourselves to have arrived in Scotland, quite fit and ready, in spite of the journey, to continue our search.

It is believed that all the Holy wells in Scotland were Pin wells, for a pin was a very common form of offering made by the pilgrims, not because it was thought particularly acceptable, but simply as a thing within reach of all. The same superstition of walking round the wells a certain number of times sun-ways was also practised in Scotland. These solar turns are mentioned in the history of many nations; what actual virtue is attributed to them it is not easy to say, but no one turns against the sun except with the object of invoking a curse or bringing bad luck to some one or something.

Saint Anthony's Well, near Edinburgh, is probably the best known of Scottish wishing-wells. It lies underneath the overhanging crags of Arthur's Seat, close to Saint Anthony's Chapel. The stream which fills the basin of the well inspired the writer of that plaintive old song, "Oh waly, waly, up yon Bank." Which song expresses the grief of Lady Barbara Erskine, on the desertion of her husband, James, Marquis of Douglas, in the time of Charles II. The last verse, so quaint and sad, gives us a pin and says :—

> "But had I wist, before I kissed,
> That love had been sae ill to win,
> I'd locked my heart in a case of gold
> And pinned it wi' a siller pin."

Another well on the borders of Dunottar, near Stonehaven, was known formerly as Saint Ninian's Well; now, merely as the Pin Well. It unfortunately went dry some years ago and has not been repaired. Up to that time it was visited on May Day morning by hosts of young folks who wished their wishes and dropped in their pins. It was not supposed to have any virtue except on May Day. The proprietor intends, we are told, to have the well repaired, when no doubt the custom will be revived.

Saint John's Well, at Balmano, Kincardineshire, still exists, though it is now also out of repair and is no longer public; but pins used to be dropped into it by the sick and wounded, who were restored by its waters.

Near the top of a hill that divides the Glen of Corgarff from Glengairn, Aberdeenshire, lies Tobar-na-glas-a-coile, i.e. "the well in the grey wood," named after a spiteful spirit that lived close by and was called Duine-glase-beg, i.e. "the little grey man." He was the guardian of the well, and most assiduous in watching over it. Each person on drinking the water had to drop in a pin; if this was not done, and the same person returned to take water a second time, the little grey man, in revenge, hunted and persecuted him until at last he died of thirst. An equally sad fate awaits careless visitors to a well at the top of Ben Newe in Strathdon, Aberdeenshire. Should they neglect to put a pin or some small thing into the water before drinking it, the tradition is they will die before reaching the bottom of the hill again. Under these tragic circumstances, we are not surprised to hear that the bottom of each of these wells was often found to be strewn with pins. A visitor to Ben Newe in 1890 saw a pill-box, a flower, and several other things besides pins in the well. A great many pins were also seen there in June 1907 by a party of young people, who themselves added to the number.

At Toubir-nim-buodh, the consecrated well near St. Kilda, visitors used to lay their offerings of pins, needles, and shells upon an altar that stood close by. It was useless to touch the sacred water until invocations had been made to the spirit of the well, and as these spirits were propitious only if remembered, and generally vindictive if neglected, no one came empty-handed.

Offerings of pins were made at the well at Metherclunie, near Dufftown, on May morning, and also at the Wallack Well, and Corsmall Well at Glass in Banffshire.

Saint Mary's Well at Orton, Morayshire (Plate XIII., Illustration 2), till a few years ago continued to attract crowds of Roman Catholics on certain days, especially on the first Sunday in May. A number of pilgrims came to pray at the well and a great many pins were put into the water as offerings. The country folks in the district still visit the well on the first Sunday in May, but only in search of good luck. Pins and buttons are also still dropped in by those who worship at this church and believe that the water has healing properties, and will cure sickness. They also take the water away in bottles.

The Island of Guernsey has her Holy wells, where offerings were made as at all other wells. They still exist in many parts of the island, and are resorted to for various purposes, but principally for the cure of erysipelas, rheumatism, and glandular swellings, and inflammation or weakness of the eyes. These maladies are all called by the country people "mal de la Fontaine," and *Guernsey Folk-lore* tells us of various ceremonies which have to be observed, and without which it is useless to visit the wells. One point is curious, and differs from the ritual at most other wells—the water must be dropped on to the affected part with the *fingers*, and *not* put on with a rag, and this must be done before the patient has broken his fast for nine consecutive mornings. The well most in repute is Saint George's in the parish of Ste. Marie du Castel, of which we give an illustration (Plate XIII., Illustration 3).

There is only one Holy well in Jersey, the Fontaine S. Marc, the water of which was supposed to have curative powers, particularly for the eyes.

We might, of course, give particulars concerning many more Pin wells; for there are wells for heart-ache, wells for headache, wells for toothache, wells for lunatics, wells to cure lameness, and, we believe, one well that is bottomless! At all of them offerings of pins were made, and at many we have shewn the custom is still kept up.

It has already been said that the pins represented the more precious offerings of very ancient times, but for hundreds of years they have been thrown in or left in some receptacle beside the wells; we can there-fore speak with impunity of their use in this way as an old tradition or custom. Some of the wells had real medicinal powers, and their waters really did good without any miracle being performed, and the offerings were left in gratitude for cures already made. These offerings took different forms. A man cured of lameness would leave his crutch near the well; another, whose sores were healed, would leave the rags with which they had been bound. There must also have been occasions when people were cured of some disease or sickness that did not require crutches or bandages, and when the ever-useful pin would be thought of and thrown in. The other wells (the Pin wells) were believed to have miraculous powers of healing, and the offerings were not thank-offerings, but to propitiate and induce the presiding saint to send the pilgrims whatever might be at the moment their heart's desire. These sacred wells were held in reverence all over the British Isles and in almost every part of the world. Miss Gordon Cumming tells us of efforts vainly made to put a stop to this form of idolatry in Scotland. "Vainly did the Council of Arles, in A.D. 452, decree that 'if in any diocese any infidel either lighted torches or worshipped trees or fountains . . . he should be found guilty of sacrilege.' Vainly did other councils again and again repeat the same warning. . . . Vainly, too, did King Edgar and Canute the Great forbid the worship of the sun, moon, fountains, &c. &c.; the people clung with tenacity to all their varied forms of paganism except the worship of trees, which seems gradually to have been forgotten, or only remembered in Germany, whence we have borrowed the Yule custom of illuminating a fir-tree with offerings of candles. . . . Among the various efforts made to check well-worship in Scotland in the seventeenth century was an order from the Privy Council appointing commissioners 'to wait at Christ's Well in Menteith on the 1st of May, and to seize all who might assemble at the spring, and imprison them in Doune Castle.'"

In spite of all this we find the same customs and superstitions still lingering, even in a land of such sturdy common-sense as Scotland. But "the way of the world is to make laws and follow customs," and we ourselves confess that "there's something in that ancient superstition, which, erring as it is, our fancy loves." So the ball is kept rolling, and will roll on until, perhaps, in years to come, when the old order of things is reversed and new laws are made, some future generations may tell the world a different tale. There we must leave it; for, having proved the use of pins at sacred wells, time and space forbid further wanderings amongst them, and we must turn to other things.

# CHAPTER V

## GAMES WITH PINS

"His first quoit fell within three inches of the pin."
—CROCKETT, *Lads' Love*, chap. xviii p. 190.

A GREAT number of curious practices and customs connected with pins had nothing whatever to do with either witchcraft or superstition, good luck or bad luck, or to the curing of disease; but from very early times pins have been put to many uses besides their original one of fastening two things together. Amongst other things there were games played with pins.

English people as a rule are lovers of games, but we are not here referring to our great national out-door games, nor to chess, whist, or bridge, but to those nice little games which while away half-hours here and there in our lives, on rainy days and long winter evenings, when we are tired of reading and some other recreation becomes necessary, but it is not worth while to start anything more serious. There are already many such games, but as they are not usually of a kind that claim interest for long together, fresh ones are always welcome; and some of those played with pins, though not very exciting in themselves, are yet so quaint and curious that we venture to think even a Christmas party of elderly people trying to be merry might become almost enjoyable with them to turn to from the more laborious forms of keeping

that festival. Some of the pin games were played at
Pudsey in Yorkshire, and we have ascertained, through
the kindness of the vicar of that parish, that they
really did exist there, but have now for some years
died out.

On the morning of New Year's Day troops of
children were seen running to and fro in the streets of
Pudsey from shop to shop, where they greeted the
owners in this curious way: "Please pray nah New
Year's gift." At the drapers' shops, they were each
given a row of pins, with which they afterwards played
at several games  One popular game was called "Cover
Pin." A child deposited secretly one or any number
of pins in the palm of his hand, all the heads being
one way; and then closing the hand, the pins were
hidden from sight. A companion covered in the same
way an equal number of pins, and then said "heads"
or "heads to points." If the coverer said "heads,"
and on the hands being opened the heads were all one
way, then the coverer won the lot; but if the heads
were "heads to points"—that is, heads opposite to the
heads in the hand—then the coverer lost, unless he had
said "heads to points."

Another game was "Drop Key," and any number
could play at this game. Each player dropped a pin or
two in turn through a key, which was fixed horizon-
tally five or six inches above the table. Each player
won only so many pins as his pin or pins covered at
each drop, and so the game went on for any length of
time.

Another game was called "Flush," or "Save-all."
A small octagonal wooden roller four or five inches
long was required. Its eight sides were marked—
two sides each with ones, twos, and crosses called

PLATE XIV

3  The Fly Cage

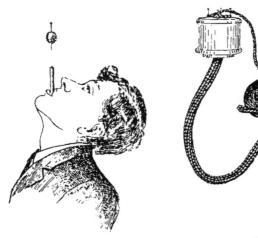

1  The Dancing Gooseberry

4  Chain made with a
Cotton Reel and Pins

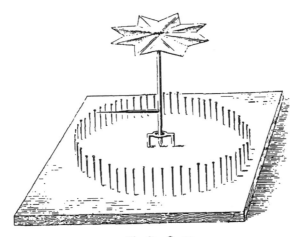

2  The Pin Organ.

"flush," and V's called "save-all." Any number could also play at this game. The players deposited two pins each; they then commenced to throw the roller in turn, and if, when the first player had thrown, it stood at one, the player took up one pin; if at two, two pins were deposited to the stock by the unlucky player; if at five, all were saved, there being neither losses nor gains; but if it stood at ten, "flush," then the thrower won the lot. It seems a pity these games should have died out, as there are now such an endless variety of pins at all prices with which to play for prizes. We can, however, give directions for playing several more games with pins, and also for making toys with pins. The "Dancing Gooseberry" was at one time a very popular game, and the "Lottery Book" was played about seventy years ago in many places.

The "Dancing Gooseberry" (Plate XIV., Illustration 1) was made by sticking a pin through a *small* gooseberry. It was then placed in the stem of a broken tobacco pipe; the pipe was placed in the mouth, and by blowing through it the gooseberry was made to dance in the air. This required great skill, as the object was to catch the gooseberry in the stem of the pipe.

"The Pin Organ" (Plate XIV., Illustration 2) is a very interesting toy, and was made in this way. A small piece of board was obtained, upon which a circle was marked out; into this circle pins were driven, and by driving them further into the wood the pins could be tuned. An upright piece of wood was then put into a support in the centre of the circle of pins. Another piece of wood with a quill at the end was then fastened into the side of the upright piece, and at the top of this upright piece was fixed a paper fan.

To use the instrument some one had to blow the fan; this caused the upright piece of wood (which was only held by its support, and not fastened) to rotate, and the quill, which touched the pins in going round, produced a series of musical notes or tunes.

"The Fly Cage" (Plate XIV., Illustration 3) was another interesting toy made from a bottle cork and pins. To make the cage a hole was cut in the centre of the cork  Pins were then fixed across the opening of the hole so as to form bars. To put the fly in, a pin was lifted out. Tormenting flies is not a thing to be encouraged, but this is a very neat toy, and we think might be put to some better use.

"Cowslip Tea." The tea was made by pouring boiling water over cowslips; sugar-candy was used to sweeten it. It was then placed in a bottle and carried about by children. A pin was paid for a spoonful.

"The Lottery Book." Pictures were placed between some (but not all) of the leaves of this book. The pictures were scraps cut from old newspapers, &c. The game was played thus: a child stuck a pin between the leaves, and if a picture was found there, he claimed it. If not, the owner of the lottery book claimed the pin.

Sixty or seventy years ago boys made musical pipes in this way: they cut reeds into lengths, and a slit was cut in the centre, which when blown into would produce a sound like the note of an organ; these were called pipes, and they were exchanged by the boys for pins, with the expression, "Who will give a pin for a pipe?" Another game, of about the same date, was called a "Children's Love Charm." The name of the lover was inscribed on a laurel leaf with a pin. If the leaf turned brown, his or her love was reciprocated, but if it turned black, was rejected.

"Tit-Tat" is an old game, and a very mischievous one. It is still played by boys on dark nights. A button, attached to a length of cotton, is suspended from the window-frame by means of a pin. By gently pulling the cotton, the button swings pendulum fashion, and causes a tapping noise on the window-pane. This game when played after dark is a most alarming experience for those on whom the trick is perpetrated, especially if they are old or nervous people. It is of course splendid fun for the players, and we can almost find it in our hearts to hope that this game may always remain fashionable.

"The Horse-Chestnut Table." This is called in some places a "conkerf," and is made of a horse-chestnut and pins, with wool wound round them in cobweb fashion.

Plate XIV., Illustration 4, shews how pins can be used with a cotton reel to make a chain. Put four pins round one of the holes of the reel at equal distances; take a ball of wool and pass the end of it through *this* hole and pull it out at the other; then twist it round each pin in turn once, and repeat the twists, so that there are two twists of wool round each pin. Lift the under twist over the upper twist, and over the pin; this must be done at each pin and *with* a pin. Then twist the wool once more round each pin, and repeat the process of lifting the under twist over the upper twist and over each pin at every round. The chain will gradually appear out of the opposite hole of the reel, and can of course be made into any length. It is a good strong chain, and we should like to see this useful and pretty occupation

F

become more general.    Many a little girl whose cry of
"What shall I do, mamma?" is so difficult to answer,
might be made quite happy and very proud if shewn
how to make a real chain; and what a charming
present it would make, when finished, for grandmamma
or aunt at Christmas.

"The Pin Dart" is composed of a pin fixed in
a small cone of paper with sealing-wax; it is used
with a paper cylinder, and naughty boys used to
tear a page from their lesson books for the purpose.
The dart is blown from the cylinder, and the point
of the pin being outwards, considerable damage
might be done if it flew into any one's face.
We are not quite sure if it is right to perpetuate
such a dangerous toy.    But if blown at a small
target made for the purpose it would then be quite a
harmless game.

Many very pretty games were played in some parts
of New England in the seventeenth and eighteenth
centuries, and Mrs Alice Morse Earle tells us much
about them in *Child-Life in Colonial Days*.    We
should like to introduce to the children of to-day
some of the charming amusements described in a
chapter of this book headed "Old-time Children."
They had such pretty ideas about flowers, and, as
many of these children were not allowed to play with
real dolls on the solemn New England Sabbath, they
made themselves dolls out of flowers.    Black-headed
dolls were made from poppies, their petals when
turned back forming bright scarlet petticoats.    The
different coloured balsams, with their "frills and
flounces," and the holyhocks, could all be tied into
tiny dolls, most fairy-like to behold; blue-bells are
shaped very much like a child's "straight-waisted, full-

skirted frock," and if pins are stuck upright in a piece of wood, the little frocks can be hung over them, and "the green calyx forms a tiny hat." Amongst other favourite amusements of these "old-time children" were "Pin-a-sights," or "Pin-shows" as they were called in England. They formed part " of the shop furnishings of pin-stores,"a kind of play-shop for which many curious articles were manufactured with pins. A "pin-a-sight" was made in this way. Flowers were stuck upon a piece of glass in different patterns. Over the flowers was pasted a piece of paper, in which was a movable flap, and on payment of a pin this flap was lifted, and the hidden treasures revealed. "Sightseers" were enticed by the children, who sang out, " A pin, a pin, a poppy show ! "—this being their rendering of a "puppet show." Tiny wreaths were made of larkspur for these " pin-a-sights," and minia-ture trees were carefully manufactured of "grass-spires." Great ingenuity could be displayed in the making of " pin-a-sights." Tiny baskets were cut in two, pasted on glass, and "filled with wonderful artificial flowers manufactured out of the petals of real blossoms." A gorgeous blue rose could be made from the petals of a flower-de-luce, &c. &c. Mrs. Earle adds a touch of pathos to these delightful reminiscences when she relates being present at the opening of an old chest which had not been searched for many years " In a tiny box within it was found some cherished belong-ings of a little child who had died in the year 1794. Among them was a tea-set made of rose-hips, with handles of bent pins." No wonder such dainty toys were amongst a little child's most " cherished belong-ings," and doubtless many bitter tears were dropped into the tiny cups by those loving friends who so carefully packed them away more than a hundred years ago.

"Pin-shows" were made in England a century ago, and for many years after. They came in each year as regularly as marbles, kites, and other games when "April showers" had brought forth "May flowers." They were made in much the same way as those described by Mrs Earle. A piece of glass was found, and laid on a piece of paper of any colour. On the glass were laid, face downwards, such small flowers as the forget-me-not, daisy or buttercup, violet or pimpernel, with here and there a small leaf. Round the glass and close to the edge were placed the petals of larger flowers, such as those of the wild-rose or foxglove, the object being to cover the whole of the glass. The sides of the sheet of paper were then carefully folded over the flowers; but in order to make the whole stronger, it was better before folding the sheet of paper to lay on the flowers a piece of stout paper or cardboard, and on this to fold the paper, which was either pinned or sewn to make the back tight and firm. The next thing was to cut the paper which covered the front of the glass, on three sides, so that the uncut side formed a flap. The "pin-show" was now ready for those who would give a pin to see it. "Please will you give me a pin to look at my pin-show?" was the children's cry, and if a pin was forthcoming, the floral show was exhibited. In this way girls gathered a great quantity of pins, which they usually handed to their mothers, for mothers in those days instilled into the minds of their children the notion of being what was called "pin-thrifty," and to pick up a pin whenever and wherever one was seen lying.

They were told :—

> "To steal a pin
> It is a sin",

and also—

> "Who see a pin
> An' let it lie,
> May want a pin
> Before they die";

or—

> "May come to want
> Before they die"

This was useful teaching in the way of thriftiness, and in all probability was the foundation of the children's pastime of making "pin-shows."

We must now turn our attention to games of quite a different kind. Some of them are very ancient, and some long since forgotten, but that well-known old book, *Sports and Pastimes of the People of England*, by Joseph Strutt, published 1831, tells us they were mostly played with wooden pins; and that bowls is one of our oldest games, probably an invention of the Middle Ages. It has been traced back to the thirteenth century, but the time of its first introduction cannot be ascertained  Strutt also gives us some valuable particulars concerning kales, closh, loggats, ninepins, skittles, half-bowl, &c., and we will now describe these games in his own words.

"Kayles," "written also cayles and keiles, derived from the French word *quilles*, was played with pins, and no doubt gave origin to the modern game of ninepins; though, primitively, the kayle-pins do not appear to have been confined to any certain number . . . the pastime kayles is played with six pins. . .  The arrangement of the kayle-pins differs greatly from that of the ninepins, the latter being placed upon a square frame in three rows, and the former in one row only."

The game "Cloish," or "Closh," "mentioned frequently in the ancient statutes, seems to have been the same as kayles, or at least exceedingly like it; cloish was played with pins, which were thrown at with a bowl instead of a truncheon, and probably differed only in name from the ninepins of the present time."

"Loggats." "This, I make no doubt, was a pastime analogous to kayles and cloish, but played chiefly by boys and rustics, who substituted bones for pins. 'Loggatts,' says Sir Thomas Hanmer, one of the editors of Shakespeare, 'is the ancient name of a play or game, which is one of the unlawful games enumerated in the thirty-third statute of Henry VIII.: it is the same which is now called kittle-pins, in which the boys often make use of bones instead of wooden pins, throwing at them with another bone, instead of bowling.' Hence Shakespeare, in *Hamlet*, speaks thus: 'Did these bones cost no more the breeding, but to play at loggatts with them?' And this game is evidently referred to in an old play entitled *The Longer thou Livest, the more Fool thou Art*, published in the reign of Queen Elizabeth, where a dunce boasts of his skill 'at skales and the playing with a sheepes-joynte.' In skales, or kayles, the 'sheepes-joynte' was probably the bone used instead of a bowl."

"Ninepins-Skittles." "The kayle-pins were afterwards called kettle or kittle-pins, and hence, by an easy corruption, skittle-pins, an appellation well known in the present day. The game of skittles as it is now played differs materially from that of ninepins, though the same number of pins are required in both. In performing the latter, the player stands at a distance settled by mutual consent of the parties concerned, and casts the bowl at the pins; the contest is, to beat them all down in the fewest throws In playing at skittles there is a double exertion: one of bowling and the other by tipping; the first is performed at a given distance, and the second standing close to the frame upon which the pins are placed, and throwing the ball through in the midst of them; in both cases, the number of pins beaten down before the return of the bowl, for it usually passes beyond the frame, are called fair, and reckoned to the account of the player; but those that fall by the coming back of the bowl are said to be foul, and of course not counted. One chalk or score is reckoned for every fair pin, and the game of skittles consists in obtaining thirty-one chalks precisely, less loses, or at least gives the antagonist a chance of winning the game; and more requires the player to go again for nine, which must also be brought exactly, to secure himself."

The preceding quotation from Hanmer intimates that the kittle-pins were sometimes made with bones, and this assertion is strengthened by the language of a dramatic writer, the author of *The Merry Milk-maid of Islington*, in 1680, who makes one of his characters speak thus to another: "I'll cleave you from the skull to the twist, and make nine skittles of the bones."

"Four Corners" "is so called from four large pins which are placed singly at each angle of a square frame. The players stand at a distance, which may be varied by joint consent, and throw at the pins a large, heavy bowl, which sometimes weighs six or eight pounds. The excellency of the game consists in beating them down by the fewest casts of the bowl."

"Half-bowl." "This is one of the games prohibited by Edward IV., and received its denomination from being played with one half of a sphere of wood. Half-bowl is practised to this day (1831) in Hertfordshire, where it is commonly called rolly-polly, and it is best performed upon the floor of a room, especially if it be smooth and level. There are fifteen small pins of a conical form required for this pastime, twelve of which are placed at equal distances upon the circumference of a circle of about two feet and a half diameter; one of the three remaining pins occupies the centre, and the other two are placed without the circle at the back part of it, and parallel with the bowling place, but so as to be in line with the middle pin; forming a row of five pins, including two of those upon the circumference. In playing this game, the bowl when delivered must pass above the pins and round the end-pin, without the circle, before it beats any of them down; if not, the cast is forfeited; and, owing to the great bias of the bowl, this task is not very readily performed by such as have not made themselves perfect by practice. The middle pin is distinguished by four balls at the top, and, if thrown down, is reckoned for four towards the game; the intermediate pin upon the circle, in the row of five, has three balls, and is reckoned for three; the first pin without the circle has two balls, and is counted for two; and the value of all the others singly is but one. Thirty-one chalks complete the game, which he who first obtains is the conqueror. If this number be exceeded it is a matter of no consequence: the game is equally won."

"Push-pin," Strutt says, "is a very silly sport, being nothing more than simply pushing one pin across another." It has, however, the distinction of having been mentioned by Shakespeare in *Love's Labour's Lost*, Act iv. sc. 1, "And Nestor played at push-pin with the boys." Strutt also gives the following amusing description under the heading of "Burlesque Music": "The minstrels and joculators seem to have had the knack of converting every kind of amusement into a vehicle of merriment, and, amongst others, that of music has not escaped them. Here we see one of these drolls holding a pair of bellows by way of a fiddle, and using the tongs as a substitute for the bow. Another man played upon the frying-pan and gridiron. I have heard an accompaniment to the violin exceedingly well performed with a rolling-pin and a salt-box by a celebrated publican called Price, who kept 'The Green Man,' formerly well known by the appellation of 'The Farthing Pye House,' at the top of Portland Row, Saint Marylebone."

"The Farthing Pye House" is a curious name for a public-house, but the names of public-houses are not usually given without a reason, and farthing pies were probably at one time sold at "The Farthing Pye House." We also often find public-houses named after the lord of the manor, as for instance "The Earl of March," in compliment to the Duke of Richmond. The aim of the sign is, of course, to draw customers, and so a national hero or a great battle are often made use of, such as "The Duke of Wellington," "The Waterloo," or "The Alma." Loyalty also shews itself at "The Crown," "The Prince of Wales," and so on.

Other signs show the speciality of their house, as " The Bowling Green," " The Skittles," &c. &c., and there are some that refer more directly to the pins with which these games are played ; thus, we find in the outskirts of Wokingham, Berks, a small wayside inn with this sign, " The Pin and Bowl." There is no pictorial illustration of it on the signboard, and the question has been asked, " Why is ' pin ' here in the singular? " It is, however, only in one sense that the word " pins " in this connection is ever used. Skittles are certainly played with " ninepins," and " bowls " also, but only in speaking of the individuals are " pins " so called. To " set up the pins " is the duty of the attendant, but collectively they are " the pack." A representation, often highly coloured, of a " pin " falling from the blow of the " bowl," is still to be seen in Bristol and elsewhere on many public-house signs, usually to show that there is a " skittle-alley " within.

The order was reversed in the " Bowl and Pin," a tavern in Upper Thames Street, in 1781, where the " Cat and Fiddle Society " held their monthly meetings. A ticket of admission to one of these meetings at the " Pin and Bowl," dated 1781, is preserved in the print-room at the British Museum, in Banks' collection of admission tickets.

There was also a " Skittle and Two Pins " in Bedfordbury ; and it is especially interesting to find that the only surviving instance in London of the " Corner Pin " still exists at No. 2 Goswell Road, formerly Goswell Street, the ancient highway between London and merry Islington. To hit the " corner pin " is the aim of every skittle player, as it is the key of the situation. In a crowded carriage of the

Exeter market-train an old-fashioned farmer was once heard to call out, " Here! Maister Cornder Pin, do 'ee plaise to let in a leetle fresh air, us be most a' steefled."   The man nearest the window held the key of that situation, and therefore represented the " corner pin."

# CHAPTER VI

## PIN CUPS—A MERRY PIN—A PEEVISH PIN— A PIN BASKET

"As for the Doctor, he was quite on the merry pin."
—ANNE MANNING, *Old Chelsea Bun-House.*

ONE thing leads to another, and the references to taverns and inns made in our last chapter lead us to consider some of the terms used in connection with the beer, wine, and spirits obtained at these public houses, such as a "pin of beer" and a "merry pin." Those ancient drinking vessels called "pin-cups" or tankards, which are of great antiquity and great historical interest, will also be considered in this chapter.

But what is a "pin of beer"? It is the smallest barrel of beer, a four and a half gallon cask. In Goldsmith's *Almanack* it appears at the head of the beer measures. Whitaker takes no notice of it, and it is difficult to understand why it is called a "pin." It may be used in the diminutive sense, as it is the smallest of casks; and it has also been suggested that it somewhat resembles a skittle-pin in shape, and that it is little larger than the huge wooden "pin-tankards" it was the custom to use at old German drinking parties, when each guest drank down to a pin, generally of silver, in the side of the tankard. "Ad Pinnas bibere," *i.e.* "to drink to the pin," was an old Danish custom of drinking, which obliged every one to drink exactly to a pin fixed on the side of a wooden cup, or pay a forfeit.

The custom of drinking to a pin was common amongst our Saxon ancestors, and during the reign of King Edgar a law was enacted at the suggestion of Saint Dunstan which forced the introduction of pins into drinking-cups for the purpose of repressing drunkenness. The tankards used had eight pins set at equal distances from the top to the bottom inside. They held two quarts, therefore there was half a pint between each pin. By the rules of good fellowship each person was to stop drinking only at a pin, and if he drank beyond it, was to drink to the next one. By this means those unaccustomed to measure their draughts were obliged sometimes to drink the whole tankard. Hence, when a person was a little elevated with liquor, he was said to have drunk to a " merry pin."

> " No song, no laugh, no jovial din
> Of drinking wassail to the pin "
> —LONGFELLOW'S *Golden Legend*.

No doubt the pins were started with the good intention of preventing people drinking more than was good for them ; but the difficulty of being able to " nick the pin," *i.e.* to drink *just* to the pin, and being compelled to drink to the next one when this was not done, made the remedy worse than the disease ; for, whilst any person able to " nick the pin " was not likely to become a " merry one," on the other hand, those unable or unwilling to do so might empty the tankard by the " rules of good fellowship," and drink to a " merry pin " indeed. From preventive it became incentive, and got worse and worse till, in 1102, Anselm, Archbishop of Canterbury, had to condemn a practice originally intended to insure moderation. Dr. Milner thinks King Edgar would not have attempted to force the law of putting pins in drinking-cups upon the nation at large unless the people had been in some degree prepared by seeing it already observed in their different religious communities. And again, when Archbishop Anselm condemned that practice, we learn that priests were also forbidden to drink *at* or *to* the pin—"nec ad Pinnas bibant." It seems, therefore, that hard drinking amongst priests was very general, those who started the pins, and those who put a stop to them, turning first to their own religious communities to enforce the laws.

Dutch drinking-cups, usually of wood, had one pin about the middle, and we have already observed that a forfeit was incurred by those who stopped drinking above or below it. It is possible that the first pin-cups in Great Britain had also but one pin in the middle, and that in later days they were divided into eight parts. Opinions differ on this point, and it is difficult to know which is the right one; but it seems to be thought that hard drinking was introduced into England from Holland, Denmark, and other northern countries, and so it is quite likely that the pin custom existed there also at a very early date; and as these northern countries are accused of introducing the evil, it would be pleasant to give them the credit of also inventing a remedy (though it did end in failure!), thus preserving the "entente cordiale" with our northern neighbours, and the peace of the world in general, which might otherwise have been endangered by these insinuations! That hard drinking was introduced from northern countries is probable from the derivations of many of the expressions used in the carousing. "Half-seas over," as applied to a state of drunkenness, originated from "op-zee," which in Dutch means (literally) "over-sea," and Gifford informs us that it was a name given to a stupefying beer introduced into England from the Low Countries, hence "op-zee" or "over-sea." The word "carouse," according to Gifford, is derived from the name of a large glass called a "rouse," in which a health was given, the drinking of which by the rest of the company formed a "carouse." Or, according to Blount's *Glossographia*, from the Old German words "gar" (all), and "ausz" (out). so that to drink "garaux" is to drink "all out," hence "carouse." It is necessary to add that there could be no "rouse" or "carouse" unless the glasses were emptied.

A very fine specimen of these pin-cups, of undoubtedly Saxon work, formerly belonging to the Abbey of Glastonbury, is now in the possession of the Dowager Lady Arundell of Wardour. It holds two quarts, and formerly had eight pins inside, dividing the liquor into half-pints. The four uppermost pins remain, and the holes from which the other four have fallen can be plainly seen. The cup is of oak, its full height with the lid being eight inches, its diameter six inches, and depth inside about six inches. The whole has been lacquered with a strong varnish, which has no doubt greatly contributed to its preservation. On the lid is carved a crucifix, with the Virgin and St. John on either side of the cross. The knob on the top of the handle, intended to raise the cover with, represents a bunch of grapes.

Round the body of the cup are carved the figures of the twelve apostles, whose names are inscribed on labels under their respective figures. Each figure holds an open

book in his hand, excepting St. Peter, who bears a key;
St. John, who supports a chalice; and Judas Iscariot,
who grasps a purse.    Under the names of the apostles
are seen birds, beasts, and flowers of different kinds, and
under these again, serpents, their heads joined, in twos,
thus producing the appearance of strange monsters.
Dr. Milner, from whose article on this cup in *Archæo-
logia*, written in 1793, we obtain our information, says
that he can discover no consistent meaning in these
last-mentioned ornaments; he therefore attributes
them to the fancy of the artist.

Three lions couchant form the feet upon which
the cup stands, and descend an inch below the body
of it.    It is thought that the reason lions were so
often adopted by our ancestors as the supporters
of thrones, statues, and a variety of other things,
is in consequence of their having been used to
support the throne of Solomon; this we learn in
1 Kings x. 19-20.    In a letter dated 10th June 1793,
from Lord Arundell, the following is taken: "This
cup is said to have been brought to Wardour Castle
from the antient Abbey of Glassenbury, and is
one of the very few things which were saved at the
destruction of that antient structure" (in 1540).    Dr.
Milner further explains that it was natural at the
destruction of the monasteries that their inhabitants
should have entrusted such valuable and curious
effects as had escaped the plunder of the commissioners
to their friends in the neighbourhood, in hopes of
better times.    So it is more than likely that by this
means the cup came into the possession of the
Arundell family, who had not changed their religion,
and one branch of which was then settled at Wardour.
The cup was again saved to the Arundells in the

great rebellion. For in May 1663 Sir Edward
Hungerford, the rebel commander in the west, and
Colonel Strode with an army of 1300 men summoned
Blanch, Lady Arundell, to surrender the plate belonging to the family and allow the castle to be searched
for this purpose. She refused to comply with this
request, and with twenty-five fighting men stood the
siege for nine days  When obliged to surrender she
kept the cup, and on retiring to Winchester at
the death of her husband she took it with her,
and kept it as long as she lived. With the exception
of the pins, the cup is as perfect as when it first came
from the workman's hands ; but several reasons are
given by Dr. Milner for presuming that this tankard
was used in the Abbey of Glastonbury before the
Norman Conquest. One reason he gives is, that with
the exception of three, whose proper emblems are
traced from scripture itself, the apostles have not the
distinctive marks which from about the eleventh or
twelfth centuries are generally affixed to their figures.
Another reason is that each of the apostles' figures is
placed under a circular arch, which being indented in the
under part, in a zigzag manner, and surmounted with
a kind of tortuous moulding, seems to bespeak a true
Saxon origin. Long hair and long beards, especially
amongst ecclesiastical personages, Dr. Milner also considers to have been much more common in the time of
the Saxons than after the Norman invasion ; and the
letters which compose the inscriptions are as old as the
tenth or eleventh centuries, if not older. They consist
entirely of Roman characters, and must be coeval with
the Conquest, about which time the Roman capitols,
Dr. Milner says, degenerated into the Gothic.

This splendid cup with all its associations makes

G

a strong appeal to the imagination, for, through all the length of years that have passed away since the time of King Edgar and St. Dunstan, Glastonbury Abbey, now in ruins, remains to this day a place of immense historical interest. It is through the kindness of its present owner that we are able to give illustrations (Plate XV, Illustrations 1 and 2) of this interesting and historical relic, to which time seems but to add fresh beauty, and which can never cease to be the wonder and admiration of all.

Plate XV., Illustrations 3 and 4, also represent a pin tankard, beautifully carved. Round the body of the cup, under four arches supported by pillars, we find the following scriptural subjects: Samson reclining in the lap of Delilah, who is cutting his hair, and a Philistine is seen approaching, carrying a coil of rope and an axe; Samson carrying off the gates of Gaza; the faithful spies, bearing a large bunch of grapes on a pole; and Joseph with Potiphar's wife. The handle of the cup represents a nude female figure, wearing a ram's horned mask in place of a fig-leaf. Her feet are hidden in the neck of a ram, into which they are thrust up to the ankles.

This cup stands upon four lions couchant, and there is a fifth lion at the top of the handle. The cover has a figure of Bacchus upon it, astride a cask, holding a cup and flagon in his hands. The carving is much finer and more finished than that of the Glastonbury cup, but has not the same rugged grandeur. Little or nothing is known of its history, and the present owner, who bought it at Christie's from the collection of the late Sir Isaac Lyon Goldsmid some years ago, believes it to be about 200 years old. The cup is 5½ inches high by 6¼ inches in diameter;

PLATE XV

1  The Glastonbury Pin-cup
(Height with lid, 8 in.,
diameter 6 in.)

2  The Glastonbury Pin cup, shewing
the Pins

3  Carved Wooden Pin cup  (Height
without lid, 5½ in., diameter,
5¼ in.)

4  Carved Wooden Pin cup, shewing the Pins

depth inside, 5¼ inches. It is made of lignum vitæ and there are six pins inside.

Another of these wooden pin-cups was bought at Yarmouth and presented to Dr. Pegge, an antiquarian who died in 1796. It is carved with scriptural subjects—Solomon enthroned, with the Queen of Sheba before him; Absalom suspended from a tree, and Joab on horseback thrusting a spear through his side; David appears above playing on a harp; Jacob's dream, &c. &c. On the rim over the figures are inscriptions relating to them, and on the lid a representation of Abraham entertaining the three angels.

The late Mrs. Baxendale, of Blackmoor End in Hertfordshire, had a silver cup with six silver pins inside it, dated about 1400. There is also a silver pin-cup in the Victoria and Albert Museum at South Kensington, said to be Dutch, and a considerable number of ancient maple-wood tankards of this kind exist in the Museum of the Royal Castle of Rosenberg at Copenhagen.

There is one other reference to pin-cups which must not be omitted. On the river Medway, five reaches below the town of Chatham, there is a portion of the river which was at one time called "Pin-cup." The reach thus named is the shortest on the river, and we presume that this fact suggested its name. It is now usually spoken of as "Pine Reach."

Pin-cups have long passed out of use, and pin measures are no more, but the expressions connected with them still remain, and the phrase "to put in the pin," meaning to refrain from drinking, is evidently in allusion to the row of pins in tankards. The original sense apparently having been lost sight of, it is now applied merely to any habit or course of conduct which it is desirable should be stopped : as, "To put in the pin at New Year," *i e.* to turn over a new leaf ; "He had two or three times resolved to . . . put in the pin " (Mayhew's *London Labour and London Poor*, 1. 345.)

Still another phrase derived from the custom of the peg tankard is "to peg out," or "pin out"—he who in drinking was overcome by too many pegs, or pins, and succumbed to their influence, being said to be "pegged " or "pinned out." Before this stage was arrived at the convivial were said, by having another peg, "to screw themselves up a peg," in the event of being a "peg too low " ·—

> "Come, old fellow, drink down to your peg !
> But do not drink any further, I beg."
> —LONGFELLOW, *Golden Legend*, iv.

To take a man down a peg is another old saying, which meant to drink at one draught enough liquor to uncover one more peg than his neighbour.

Halliwell, in his *Dictionary of Archaic and Provincial Words*, explains the phrase " on the pin " as = on the qui vive ; "in a merry pin," *i.e.* a merry humour. L'Estrange uses the word " pin " for a "note" or " strain "; it is not unlikely that the phrase "in a merry pin " may have been used for "in a merry key" or "strain "

It has been suggested that Cowper in his poem "John Gilpin " did not mean it in this sense when he wrote—

> "The calender, right glad to find
> His friend in merry pin."

It is, however, impossible to accuse our old friend
John Gilpin of having drunk to a merry pin, for—

> "The bottles twain behind his back
> Were shatter'd at a blow";

and—

> "Down ran the wine into the road,
> Most piteous to be seen."

Cowper must have meant here that the dear old
fellow, in spite of all his trials on that disastrous day,
was still able to appear in a merry humour, or, as his
friend put it, "in a merry pin." This same phrase
is very frequently met with in the seventeenth century,
meaning "high jinks," "larking."

> "Hark, how the frothy, empty heads within
> Roar and carouse ith' jovial Sin,
> Amidst the wilde Levalto's on their merry Pin"
>
> —BENLOWE'S *Theophila* (1652).

> "My Lady and her Maid upon a merry pin
> They made a match"
>
> —*Antidote against Melancholy* (1661)

"As the woman was upon the peevish pin, a poor
body comes, while the forward fit was upon her, to
beg" (L'Estrange) This is a very quaint rendering
of "pin humour."

In case our readers are "pegged out," or "a peg
too low," after hearing so much about pins, of which
subject they may well by now be weary; and as we
hope they will, like John Gilpin, bravely endeavour
to bear up through all the mazes of this inexhaustible
subject, and like him maintain a "merry pin" until
the end, we must ask them to "screw themselves up
a peg," as there is still much to say, and we cannot
yet "put in the pin." We can only give it different

form and convert the "merry pin" into the "pin-basket."

This curious term was used by our ancestors in connection with the youngest child of a family; the child was called the "pin-basket," and at the present time we believe it to be not quite out of use as an expression. According to our dictionaries the "pin-basket" is the youngest child of a family, and in a French dictionary we have seen it explained by simply the word "Benjamin." The mother's youngest child is called the "pin-basket," because the basket containing the infant toilet remains thereafter pinned up and closed. The term was, however, certainly at one time made use of to express having finished or "done with a thing," and in this sense it is undoubtedly meant in the following quotations :—

"But, as children used to keep their plumbs to the last, so our author (after all his preliminary reasons) hath kept the Will of King Henry the Eighth as a stone in his sleeve, for the *pin-basket*, or clencher, to all the rest." (*The Succession of the House of Hannover, Vindicated*, &c. (edition 1714), p. 4.)

"I find he has met with something he is mighty fond of, and hath made it his *pin-basket* of instances." (*The Pretender's Declaration Abstracted*, &c. (1715), p 17.)

"As a *pin-basket*, or murdering stroke to Christianity," &c. (*Asgill upon Woolston*, 1730.)

"And I do also believe that this expression is now calculated to be the last of the exceptions as the *pin-basket* upon me of what I can neither answer nor excuse." (*Defence*, &c. (1712), p. 56.)

Peasants in Wales are sometimes heard to say, "I will put a pin in her basket." By which they mean, in the vulgar tongue, "I will do for the chap," "I will finish him off," "I will cook his hash for him."

There is an interesting paragraph from Miss Eleanor Hayden's *Travels Round our Village* which illustrates that rendering of the term pin-basket which means "finished," or "done with," or "the last of a thing": "In some villages it is still the custom to bring the feast week to a close by a second dance on the last evening; this, in local phraseology, is styled 'pinning up' the feast, and the process attracts many villagers from the surrounding villages. I have been often told that Mary, or Emily Jane, is gone to 'pin up the feast,' at such and such a place; and much perplexed I was at first by this mysterious expression."

It is strange to find old-fashioned traditions and expressions clinging like ivy to some places, whilst in others they seem never to have been heard of, or else to have been quite forgotten. Many of them are handed down from father to son, orally, and as there must in some generations be people who do not adhere to this rule, or whose memories are not good, a link in the chain is thus broken and a gap made which is never repaired; and so, gradually, the thing dies out altogether, and the old customs, traditions, and expressions are swept away by that resistless current which Spencer has called "the ever-whirling wheel of change." Goldsmith says, "I love everything old—old friends, old times, old manners, old books, old wines," and we are told that King James used to call for his old shoes, as they were easier for his feet! Our readers will agree with King James, and we all find it pleasant occasionally to visit some retired spot which still rests in the calm waters of its old traditions. Here we may also call for our old shoes, and still find people who talk of " pinning up the feast," a " pin-basket," and a thousand other things of which history makes no mention.

# CHAPTER VII

## TIRLING-PINS—DOOR-PINS—ROLLING-PINS

" O he has run to Darlinton.
And tirled at the pin "—*Prince Robert*, IX

WE must now carry our readers off in search of yet
another kind of pin, and as this must be done as speedily
as possible, for time flies, let us for once imagine
ourselves to have a witch's privilege of flying through
the air on a broomstick, and thus be transported to
the " Old Town " in Edinburgh. We will then hunt
among the oldest houses, and examine the entrance
doors, where it is said the " tirling-pin " may sometimes still be found ; though about the year 1765
knockers were very generally substituted for them,
in this and other large towns, as being more genteel.

The tirling-pin is a Scotch invention of the olden
time, and was formed of a small square rod of iron
twisted or otherwise notched, which was placed perpen-
dicularly, starting out a little from the door, and bearing
a small ring of the same metal, which those who desired
admittance drew rapidly up and down the nicks or
twists so as to make a grating sound   The ring could
be tirled lightly to give merely a musical tinkle,
enough to obtain attention, or it could be pulled up
and down the notches rapidly, producing sound enough
to waken the " Seven Sleepers." It is still usual in
Scotland when any one raps at the door to say that
he, or she, is " tirlin' at the door." " Tirl " (Anglicè

twirl or agitate) in Lowland Scotch is used for a rap,
a stroke, a tap ; " tirling," for the tremulous thrilling
motion produced by repeated knocks. The word
came to be used for the expedient whereby notice
was given to open a closed or locked door.

Amongst Scottish ballads allusions are made to
this relic of antiquity :—

> " And whan she cam' to Lord Beichan's yetts,
>    She tirl'd gently at the pin,
>  So ready was the proud porter
>    To let the wedding guests come in."
> —*From " Lord Beichan," an Aberdeenshire*
>    *ballad.*

Another is from " Sweet William's Ghost "—

> " There came a ghost to Marg'ret's door
>    With many a grevious groan ;
>  And aye he tirled at the pin,
>    But answer she made none "

In the next we meet our old friend the " merry pin "—

> " I hope it's nae a sin
>  Sometimes to tirl a merry pin "
>    —*From " Skinner's Miscellanies "*

We conclude this to mean that any one returning
home in a " merry pin " would tirl or rap at the
door in a way peculiar to that condition.

Burns alludes to it in " Verses Written on a
Window of the Inn at Carron "—

> " But when we tirl'd at your door
>    Your porter dought na hear us "

It is evident that " tirling the pin " in these old
ballads was equal to turning, lifting the latch, or
trying the door, and was not always responded to
from within.

PLATE XVI

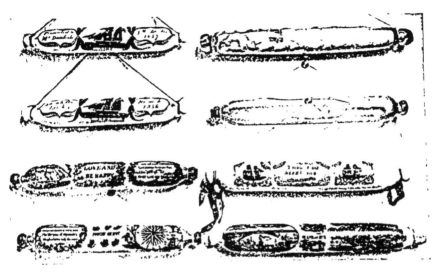

Glass Rolling-pins    (Size, 10 to 15 in. long.)

*From 80 to 100 years old*

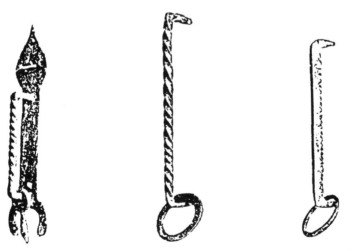

1  Tirling-pin with latch
   attached at top, and
   iron ring or hasp

2  Tirling-pin with only
   an iron ring or hasp

3  Tirling pin with only
   an iron ring or hasp

*Used in Scotland till about 1765, when knockers came into fashion*

A good description of a tirling-pin is given in *Peveril of the Peak*, when Julian seeks an entrance into the residence of his lady-love at the Black Fort in the Isle of Man : " An iron ring, contrived so as when drawn up and down to rattle against the bar of notched iron through which it was suspended, served the purpose of knocker, and to this he applied himself."

There are two tirling-pins at John Knox's House in Edinburgh, and there is one on the door of Masterton Farm-house, Masterton Village, near Dunfermline ; with these exceptions it seems doubtful if even one remains anywhere in Scotland, though it is true some houses recently erected in Ramsay Garden, Edinburgh, have been supplied with wooden tirling-pins on their entrance doors, in imitation of the old ones.

The Society of Antiquarians of Scotland have a good collection of real iron tirling-pins at the National Museum of Antiquities in Edinburgh. Some of the more modern ones have a latch attached to the top (Plate XVI., Illustration 1), but those of an earlier date only just the iron ring or hasp (Illustrations 2 and 3, Plate XVI.), the use of which we have already described.

The only instance we can find of a tirling-pin out of Scotland was on the front door of the rectory at Ovingham-on-Tyne, in Northumberland. The present incumbent of the parish tells us that about nine years ago the front entrance of the rectory was enlarged and altered, and the old door was done away with, but the tirling-pin was preserved, and now hangs on the inside of the garden door.

It does not perhaps seem very clear why they were called *pins*. But wherever a description of them is given, they are spoken of as "an iron handle or pin inserted in a door," or as "a pin, or risp, on the door." Also as "the upright pin which answers to the handle." The handle is certainly the "pin," and as the oldest tirling-pins were merely staples— a staple being a bar bent and driven in at both ends, the ends being sharpened to a point for this purpose (see Illustrations 2 and 3, Plate XVI.)—we suppose this must be the reason they were originally called tirling-pins.

The primitive door-latch in time took the place of the tirling-pin, and may still be seen in very old cottages where the wooden bar inside is lifted by a wooden lever which projects outside. Callers used to rattle this up and down to attract attention. This was superseded with a latch lifted by a string, which had to be carefully handled, and would not bear much rattling. Then came the more pretentious knocker.

So again we find old fashions cast off for new ones, and the knocker (though it cannot be said to be quite out of fashion) is now seldom seen, and still more seldom used, even by the postman. The shrill note of an electric bell is gradually taking the place of all other methods of obtaining admittance to a house, and we find it at present a most excellent invention. But, who knows, when another hundred years have passed away it will probably have fallen into disuse like the tirling-pin, and some contrivance, undreamt of now, be established in its place.

A "door-pin" was used in Derbyshire more than fifty years ago, but, unlike the tirling-pin, which was meant to assist people to enter a house, the "door-pin" was used to prevent their entrance. When a gossip was out chattering with her neighbours she would fasten down the door-latch from the outside with a piece of wood called a door-pin, this being an understood notice that she was from home, and the house must not be entered by callers. This pin is also a thing of the past, but we must not forget the "rolling-pin," still a familiar article in our kitchens. It has its poetical aspect, and once upon a time a certain baroness (her name is not revealed) had the "arms" of her husband emblazoned upon the kitchen rolling-pin with which his pastry was prepared, thus transforming this prosaic article.

Glass rolling-pins are, however, very pretty things, and many of our readers will have seen them hanging up in cottages, especially near the sea, for they were usually a sailor's charm, given to his sweetheart, or received from her before starting on a voyage, to secure "good luck." The sailor would hang the rolling-pin in his cabin, and no doubt derived great comfort from its presence, especially if it was by chance adorned with such touching words as "Think on me."

A great many glass rolling-pins have found their way into the midland counties, and the eight specimens shewn in Plate XVI., Illustration 4, come from in or near Worksop. Nos. 1 and 2 were in the first place given by sailors to their wives or sweethearts before starting on a long voyage, presumably in the good ship *Jane*, of which ship there is a fine portrait upon the rolling-pin. No. 3 has the motto "Love and be Happy," with a wreath of roses and leaves round it. On the left of the words we see a ship in full sail; below the ship the words

"Great Australia," and on the right these lines
appear—

> "From rocks and sounds and barren lands
>     Kind fortune keep me free,
>   And from great guns and women's tongues
>     Good Lord deliver me!"

No. 4 has in the centre the words "Forget me
not," with three roses above and three below them.
Set in a wreath of leaves, on the left is this verse—

> "Sweet, oh sweet is that sensation
>     When two hearts in union meet,
>   But the pain of separation
>     Mingles bitter with the sweet"

On the right is a ship, almost entirely hidden by a
compass. Below the ship are the words, "Come box
the compass," surrounded by a wreath of roses.

No. 5 is a beautiful specimen of the art of blowing glass in two colours, and No. 6 hangs in a cottage
at Worksop, and was sent to its owner on her wedding
day more than fifty years ago. It has hung in the
same place ever since, used only on special occasions
to prepare pastry for weddings or birthdays. When
first presented, this rolling-pin was filled with the best
tea that was then procurable, and if it was the old
gunpowder sort, then the contents would weigh one
pound, and the value would be perhaps 7s. 6d. At
the present time it is filled with sand.

No. 7 has the words "Thou God see'st me" in
the centre, and on either side appears a ship in full
sail.

No. 8 is a "Token of love," and a large rose set
in leaves is placed above the words; on the left, below
the words, is a view of a bridge with ships passing
under it. There are clouds above the bridge, and

above the clouds the words, " An east view of the New Bridge, Sunderland."

This rolling-pin was made at one of the glass-works in the north of England, and so were Nos 1 and 2. Nos. 3 and 4 are the oldest, and were made at Bristol about one hundred years ago. Nos. 5 and 6 were made in Yorkshire seventy or eighty years ago. No. 7 was also made at Bristol, but it is not so old as Nos. 3 and 4.

The rolling-pins were generally loaded with either sand or salt, and they were from ten to fifteen inches long, and four or five inches in circumference.

The *Connoisseur* of June 1911 has a delightful article on " Nailsea Glass," by H. St. George Gray, from which we learn many interesting particulars concerning glass rolling-pins ; the illustrations shew specimens described by Mr. Gray as having been blown into almost every colour of the rainbow. He tells us they were sometimes sixteen inches long, and occasionally filled with flour.

# CHAPTER VIII

## PIN-PRICKT PICTURES—MARIE ANTOINETTE'S PIN-PRICKT LETTER

"Could Time, his flight reversed, restore the hours
When, playing with thy vestures' tissued flowers,
The violet, the pink, and jessamine,
I prick'd them into paper with a pin"
—COWPER, *Lines on the Receipt of my Mother's Picture*

AN interesting pastime, much enjoyed by some of our ancestors, exhibits the pin as an instrument capable of producing really artistic work, and gives yet another turn to this seemingly inexhaustible subject; we refer to pin-prickt pictures. These charming pictures are very rare, and strangely little is known of their history, but they are believed to be mostly of English make, and some are quite two hundred years old. A wonderful variety of design and composition is shewn in the making of them, and with the addition of a little water-colour painting they assume quite a decorative character. The borders of flowers and leaves, partly prickt and partly coloured, are extremely delicate and dainty, and when forming a framework to figures in picturesque costume, the whole effect is most pleasing. Some are merely quaint, but all are of interest as shewing the kind of elaborate and laborious work with which our ancestors were wont to vary the monotony of their daily lives  From the introduction to Mr. Andrew Tuer's *Old-fashioned Children's Book*, a collection and reprint of many little books familiar in early days, we quote the following : " Pricking pictures with pins was another agreeable accomplishment. The pins were of several thicknesses, broad lines and heavy shadows being prickt on paper with stout, and the finer work with thin pins. A toothed wheel with sharp points was used for outlines. For filling up large spaces two or more wheels were mounted on one axle. Without such labour-saving appliances, the more ambitious and microscopically minute pin-prickt pictures, specimens of which survive, could not have been achieved." This must have been very elaborate work, and a simpler method is described in *The Young Ladies' Book : a Manual of Elegant Recreations, Exercises, and Pursuits.*

" Piercing Costumes on Paper." " Turkish or other figures, in oriental costume or draperies, are produced by a combination of water-colour painting for the features, with a series of small punctures made with needles of various sizes for the dresses. The face, hands, and feet being first drawn and coloured, the outline and folds of the drapery are marked with a tracing needle ; the paper is then laid upon a piece of smooth cloth, or a few sheets of blotting-paper, and the punctures inserted in the folds of the dress from the front to the back of the paper ; the drawing is then laid with its surface downwards, and the interior of the various outlines filled up with punctures made with a very fine needle, from the back to the front of the paper. It sometimes affords a pleasing variety if the costume be wholly or partially coloured, as it relieves the monotony of the white. Needles of various sizes should be used at discretion, and the whole of the background or body of the paper painted in some sober opaque colour to throw up the figure."

H

From this it would appear that needles were sometimes used instead of pins, but the pins were more convenient to hold, and must, we think, have been the recognised instruments for this work, though perhaps where very fine pricks were required, needles might be useful.

After a careful examination of those pin-prickt pictures we have been so fortunate as to come across, we think the last method described, from *The Young Ladies' Book*, must be correct. The whole design in each picture appears to be outlined with rather larger pricks, done from the front to the back, and all the filling up (of spaces) is prickt from the back to the front of the paper, as though following the directions given. We see no reason why anything but a pin, or perhaps a needle for the very finest work, should have been used. But it is of course true that the labour with a pin alone would be very great; we must therefore admit the possibility of some other kind of tool being utilised. The pins may have been inserted into a handle; several pins might be used in this way, which would considerably lessen the labour.

Plate I., represented in our Frontispiece, might well have been done from the directions given in *The Young Ladies' Book*. It is a fine specimen of pin-pricking. The lady's face, hands, and hair are painted, as well as the back of the chair on which she is seated, and the ribbons and feathers which flutter round as though stirred by some gentle breeze. It is a clever picture, full of life, and so realistic we seem actually to see the lady's fingers pass swiftly over the harp-strings, and to hear the sound of the music she makes. The dress is entirely pin-prickt, and the

PLATE XVII

Pin-prickt Picture.  (English.)

*About two hundred years old.*

PLATE XVIII

Pin-prickt Picture (English).
*About two hundred years old.*

folds so well expressed in broad masses and fine lines, we do not miss the pencil shading or the deep shadows made with paint and brush that usually help to make a picture. The pricks express everything; is not this very wonderful? If our readers have read the directions given in *The Young Ladies' Book,* and will now examine this picture closely, they will see for themselves that by marking out the prominent folds of the dress with rather larger pricks from the front to the back of the picture, and then turning it round and placing it face downwards, and filling up all those parts between the prominent lines with small pricks put very close together from the back to the front, the folds will then stand out, making their own shadows. Plates XVII. and XVIII. are not so finely prickt as Plate I., and the design and painting of the borders is much less finished, but they are probably older, and it is believed that those pictures which have a saint painted in water-colour as their chief decoration or ornament were made from one hundred to two hundred years ago in the religious houses that were then numerous in different parts of England, especially in the eastern counties. Those which survive the ravages of time, and have descended to Roman Catholic families now living, are looked upon as very great treasures, and their owners are unwilling to part with them.

St Stephen (Plate XVII.) and St. Francis (Plate XVIII) have similar borders entirely pin-prickt and surrounded by waved lines painted in two shades of blue. Little painted bouquets of pink flowers with blue leaves are introduced. St. Stephen holds the martyr's palm, and St. Francis the cross; he wears the friar's habit of his Order, and on his hands we see the wounds which it is said appeared on them, and also on his feet, shortly before his death. They were, like those of our Saviour, continually bleeding, and after his death disappeared entirely. These two pictures are quaint and curious, and the painting of the figures shews much skill, but it is of course impossible to say if the same hand painted and prickt them.

Plate XIX. was found in a curiosity shop at San Remo; no information could be gathered from its owner excepting that it was very old. It is tinted in very delicate tones, the bow at the top being pale rose colour, and there are touches of blue here and there The face, hands, and furniture are also painted. If this figure is compared with Plate I. (Frontispiece) our readers will at once see that the folds, though marked out with larger pricks, do not stand out in the same realistic way. The whole has a flatter appearance, and there is not so much life and movement. It is very finely prickt indeed, and the light and tasteful border, a mixture of pricks and painting, deserves the highest praise. The table is rather uncomfortably out of drawing, but the floor has some attempt at perspective; and the woman, whose face is very dark, holds in her hand what appears to be the "merry-thought" bone of a chicken, thought to be a charm against drowning. She may be about to wish a wish in some mysterious way of her own, but it is a serious business, for her face betrays an anxious mind. What is the history of the picture, where it was made, and when, must be a matter of conjecture.

Plate XX. is said to be a rare and valuable specimen. The gentleman's dusky countenance proclaims him from the East, as does his oriental costume. Only

PLATE XIX

Pin-prickt Picture.

*Nationality and date unknown.*

PLATE XX

Pin-prickt Picture.

*Nationality and date unknown.*

PLATE XXI

Pin-prickt Picture (English).

*Date* 1780.

PLATE XXII

Pin-prickt Picture (English).

Date 1780.

the face and the hands of the figure are painted, and one boot which peeps from the flowing white draperies He is a busy, careful man, note the hour-glass to time his work, and see how diligently he mends his pen! The ink-pot makes us feel rather uncomfortable, and we fear it will slide off that slanting table long before the pen is ready to be dipped into it. The colouring of this picture is very crude. The chair has a bright crimson back, and black and yellow woodwork. The hour-glass is also crimson, and the table and floor are pink.

Plates XXI. and XXII. are perhaps the most beautiful examples we have been able to procure. They are a fine pair of pictures, of English make, dated 1780 Plate XXI. represents two boys at play, and might well be named "The Twins," so much alike are these pretty playmates. One boy is preparing to spin his top, whilst the other, with a whistle in his hand, anxiously awaits the happy moment when it will be flung upon the ground to hum its own particular tune over the floor. The boys' heads and hands, their shoes, sashes, and toys, and the buttons on their coats are painted, all the rest is prickt.

In Plate XXII. a little boy dressed in somewhat fantastic style is playing a violin. His face, hands, hair, and shoes are painted, as well as his violin and bow and the ribbon, feathers, and rosettes that adorn his dainty little person. Each picture is surrounded by the same lovely border, a design of leaves and stems that resemble small branches of coral; at the top is a shell-like ornament from which depend little festoons of flowers and leaves. The groundwork of each border is painted pink, with crossed lines forming little squares upon it, and a green stem twists itself through the border on each side. Every detail is beautifully and carefully rendered in colour and pricks, and these two pictures are prettier than we can describe, the colouring is so delicate and the pricking so fine, giving to the whole a most quaint and old-fashioned appearance.

The two oval pictures (Plate XXIII., Illustrations 1 and 2) contain silhouette portraits of Henry IV. of France and his friend and minister, the celebrated "Sulli." We have several times observed, in describing pin-pictures, that they were "very finely prickt." These two, however, surpass all we have seen in this respect; and what makes them still more remarkable is the fact that without the aid of pencil or brush the pictures separate themselves from the paper in clear and perfect relief, this effect being produced entirely by pin-pricks. King Henry wears a wreath of laurels, and his hair and beard are prickt into the most realistic resemblance of innumerable little curls. Every detail is well defined; one can even read the King's sinister expression. Sulli has a much pleasanter cast of countenance, and his hair, though not so abundant, is also prickt into many curls. The ruff at his neck is singularly perfect, and every part of the picture rich in detail. Particular interest is attached to these two pictures as coming from Knole, that picturesque and historical residence replete with every kind of treasure, and filled with the golden memories of those kings, queens, archbishops, and cardinals who have at different times made it their home.

We have the pleasure and honour of knowing a lady now in her 101st year, who plays the piano with great skill every day of her life, usually takes

PLATE XXIII

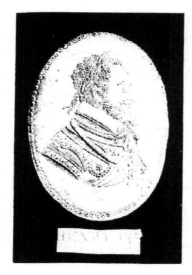 

1. Pin-prickt Silhouette Portrait
of Henry IV. of France.

*17th century.*

2. Pin-prickt Silhouette Portrait
of Sulli.

*17th century.*

3. Pin-prickt Picture. (By a lady, now living, aged 100 years.)

PLATE XXIV

a walk in the morning, and receives her numerous friends at tea-time. She remembers in her youth pricking many pictures with pins, but unfortunately they have not been preserved. However, on hearing we were interested in this charming pursuit, she set to work, undaunted by age and somewhat failing sight, and presented us with the little picture here reproduced (Plate XXIII., Illustration 3). Her method was to place the paper on which the outline of the flower had been drawn, on to a piece of soft material; she prickt the outline with a pin on the right side, and then filled up all the spaces in the flower and its leaves with pin-pricks put very close together. When it was all filled up she lifted the prickt paper and turned it round, shewing the rough side which the pins had pierced, the paper being raised by this process. This was the right side of the picture, and we feel sure all will agree that it is a wonderful piece of work for a lady of so great an age to have accomplished. The method is almost but not quite the same as that described in *The Young Ladies' Book*.

Plate XXIV. reveals a different class of pin-picture, and has for its foundation a French print, partly coloured, shewing the " Salle des Festins," at Versailles, on the occasion of a dinner given during the rejoicings for peace in 1763. The "Salle" is lighted with candles 'in chandeliers, suspended from the ceiling; there are also candles upon the tables, and each candle tip is prickt with a pin. The walls, ceiling, and outlines of the windows and door are also prickt, and when this picture is held up against the light, the " Salle des Festins " has the appearance of being brilliantly illuminated by electricity. Hours must have been spent in the making of these pictures, and they must of course have varied in beauty and design according to the skill and imagination of the worker.

There seems to be an allusion to something of the kind in Cowper's lines on the "Receipt of my Mother's Picture" which head this chapter.

Many middle-aged persons remember in their childhood being given pieces of paper on which designs had been traced with a pencil; these were placed upon a well-stuffed chair or sofa, and the design prickt out with a pin, the pin going nicely through the paper into the chair or sofa, and coming out again with a pleasing and satisfactory sound, without, we presume, doing much harm to the furniture! Something of this kind is done by children of the present day, so the art has not yet completely died out, but is not likely to be revived in its old-fashioned form. For leisure has now almost disappeared, and the hurry and rush in which we live would certainly prevent such laborious work from again becoming the fashion. A hundred, or two hundred years ago time hung more heavily, and the days we now consider far too short were then most likely far too long, and any employment, however difficult or intricate, could only have been looked upon as a welcome occupation with which to pass away many weary hours of each day. But though our lives are now enriched by other and more interesting occupations of a less laborious nature, a tender charm will ever surround the memory of those which, like pin-prickt pictures, have, alas, ceased to exist.

That beautiful but unfortunate queen, Marie Antoinette, has immortalised the pin, and given to it a romantic and almost sacred character; for, during her imprisonment, wishing to communicate with some friends who were arranging an attempt to release her, she sent them a slip of thin white paper, five inches long by one and three-quarter inches wide, on which the following words were prickt with a pin : "Je suis gardée à vue, je ne parle à personne. Je me fie à vous, je viendrai."

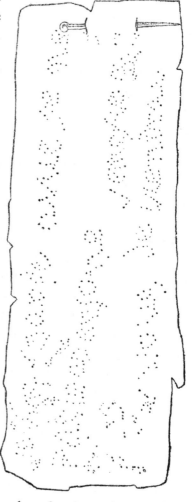

This letter, which was only deciphered in 1876 by Monsieur Pelinski, paleographer, was written to the Comte de Rougeville, who had arranged to carry off the queen and take her to the Château de Livry (Seine et Oise), where two hundred armed horsemen were waiting to conduct her into Austria.

She had no pen or pencil, and so with a pin painfully prickt out this message. But treason was at work, the message was betrayed, and all was lost. This was seven weeks before her death, and no other chance of escape was given her. By the kindness of Monsieur Dumoulin, the French publisher of *La Révolution*, par Charles D'Héricault, in which book a facsimile of this celebrated letter appears, we are enabled to give a reproduction.

The unhappy queen, deprived of everything that could occupy her fingers or her mind, is said to have also used a pin to write out a list of her linen upon the walls of the prison, thus adding another touching tribute to this useful and valuable little article, which must be honoured accordingly.

# CHAPTER IX

POLICY OF PIN-PRICKS—DEADLY HATPINS—CON-
SPIRACY OF THE BLACK-PIN—"ÊTRE TIRÉ À
QUATRE ÉPINGLES"

"That last word prickt him like a pin"
—LOWELL, *The Courtin.*

THE pathetic tale with which we ended our last
chapter does not, however, close the subject of pin-
pricks, and it is interesting to note how the pin, our
daily and hourly companion through life, has pricked
its way into everything, everywhere; and has even
become (in a figurative sense) the handle for a
political expression, in France first and afterwards
in England. The "entente cordiale" between these
countries being at the present moment so strong,
it is gratifying to find a French expression giving us
further matter for discussion on the subject. This
expression, "à coups d'épingle," is translated in
Contanseau's dictionary as "inch by inch," and
Littré's *Dictionnaire Etymologique* explains it as
"Petites offenses, petites contrariétés, que l'on inflige
à quelqu'un" Larousse's *Dictionnaire Universel* says:
"Coup d'épingle—Coup porté avec une épingle que
l'on enfonce dans la peau. Fig. Blessure légère de
l'amour propre." It evidently means a very subtle and
acute pain of an exasperating, irritating nature, which
may be administered by one person to another, and has
also been administered by one nation to another at times

of dissension and strife. As a political expression it was common in France more than a hundred years ago, but it is difficult, if not impossible, to ascertain exactly when it was first used, and by whom.

It occurs in a letter dated August 11, 1777, from De Vergennes to D'Angiviller, then Director of the French Board of Works. He proposes to suppress the words "ordered by the United States or States-General" in the description given in the Salon catalogue of a monument to General Richard de Montgomeri, who was killed at Quebec in 1775. "Ainsi," says De Vergennes, "nous évitons toute plainte, ce qui est toujours prudent, car ce ne sont jamais les coups d'épingle qui décident de la fortune des États !"

We also find it called "a classical expression in French," used by Jacques de Lille, the Virgillian poet, who was protected by Voltaire. In his poem *La Conversation*, published 1812, he wrote :—

> " J'aime à rêver, mais je ne veux pas
> Qu' à coups d'épingle on me réveille."

There are probably earlier examples of its use ; and taking the English words, in their literal sense, we can go back as far as Shakespeare for an instance :—

> " I will not swear these are my hands ; let's see ;
> I feel this pin-prick."
> —*King Lear*, Act iv. sc. 7 (written 1605).

Cormenin, a French writer (born, 1783 ; died, 1866), uses the expression in a figurative sense. This is Cormenin's quotation : " Pour moi, dût-on blâmer ce goût-là, je préfère ces militaires brutaux, qui dégainent leur sabre et qui marchent droit sur vous, à ces rhéteurs doucereux qui vous assassinent à coups d'épingle."

We entirely agree with Cormenin's views upon this subject; and who would not prefer a severe and even violent scolding which is soon over and forgotten, to the constant and exasperating nagging of those who can neither forget nor forgive.

Alphonse Daudet (born, 1840; died, 1879) evidently agrees with Cormenin, for "coups d'épingle" forms part of the title of the eleventh chapter of his *Aventures Prodigieuses de Tartarin de Tarascon.* The chapter is headed "Des coups d'épée, Messieurs, des coups d'épée. . . . Mais pas de coups d'épingle!"

In 1824 Sir Walter Scott described the chase of a hare by terriers, who "would have stuck to the chase till they had killed the hare, which would have been like being pricked to death with pins." (Lockhart's *Life of Scott.*)

This phrase is also said to occur in the official account of the meeting between Napoleon and the Czar Alexander at Tilsit on 22nd June 1807. "For the maintenance of peace," Napoleon said, "nations should avoid the pin-pricks which forerun cannon-shots." There is another instance of Napoleon having used almost the same expression when he was imprisoned at St. Helena. "Lady Malcolm, in her *Diary of St. Helena,* writes, 19th June 1817, Bonaparte said 'It was possible to live under the regulations established by Sir George (Cockburn), but now we are tortured to death by pin-point wounds.'"

Some of these quotations express such agonies of pain, they are almost Dantesque in character, and remind one of the tortures to be endured by sinners in the *Inferno.* But life is full of pin-pricks, and it seems an excellent way of expressing those small but exasperating worries with which we are constantly surrounded, which destroy vitality more slowly, but often more surely, than the sword-thrusts of greater troubles. Well may the poet sing, "What great events from little causes spring," and how often it would be wise to remember Napoleon's words and "avoid the pin-pricks which forerun cannon-shots." Thus we point a moral to adorn our tale!

The expression has certainly more power and is much more effective in French; but we are, alas! still far from knowing when it was first used, and by whom. It must have grown up with the pins in some mysterious way, for it seems as difficult to put an exact date to its birth, as it is to date the exact progress of pins from one stage of their existence to another, from their prehistoric source to the pins of to-day. "Pin-pricks" was used politically in England in 1885, and in *Le Matin* of November 8, 1898, a writer in that paper stated that ever since France refused to co-operate with England in Egypt, the French had inaugurated the policy of playing tricks on Great Britain, and that the English have at last been exasperated by the continual "pin-pricks" which have been given them.

On November 16th the *Times* referring to this article used the words "a policy of pin-pricks." *Le Temps* of November 19th had an article denying on the part of France the existence of a "politique de coups d'épingle." Other newspapers took this up, and "a policy of pin-pricks" was common talk in London during the winter of 1898.

The *Daily Mail* of 16th November 1898 had a

leading article headed "The End of the Pin-pricks":
"In his speech last night at Manchester, Mr. Chamberlain once more covered the whole field of Anglo-French relations. He saw no reason why in the future the two Powers should not be friends, but he clearly stated that no friendship is possible unless France is prepared to abandon her 'policy of pin-pricks,' as the *Matin* describes the series of petty injuries and insults which France in the last two years has inflicted upon England."

Another article appeared in the *Daily Mail* two days later, which said, "The French Government is so enamoured of its policy of pin-pricks that it is now trying it upon Italy."

Ten years after, in November 1908, this same paper had a paragraph headed "Suffragettes Disappointed," which describes an occasion on which there seems to have been some fear of a dangerous attack of pin-pricks in their literal sense, for the paragraph ends: "By order, it was understood, of Mr. (now Lord) Gladstone, women prisoners at Clerkenwell Sessions yesterday were allowed to appear in hats, but without hatpins." This speaks for itself, and it is sad to think that the precious pin is capable of becoming a really dangerous weapon; but when we speak of hatpins and hatpin pricks, most of us are now only too well aware of the painful wounds which can be inflicted by them. Germany has not escaped the hatpin peril, and an interesting little article with the tragic title of "Deadly Hatpin—Heavy Casualty List in Berlin," appeared in the *Daily Mail* of 17th December 1908. It is worth reading, and should help to free the world of this painful nuisance.

### Deadly Hatpin

HEAVY CASUALTY LIST IN BERLIN

(*From our own correspondent*)

"Berlin, *Friday.*

"A campaign against the murderous hatpin has been instituted by the newspapers of Berlin, in view of a series of accidents which have already occurred during the busy period of Christmas shopping.

"Numbers of more or less serious injuries have been caused by these dangerous implements protruding from the huge hats of fashionable ladies. Last Sunday a lady was permanently blinded in one eye when taking part in a rush at a 'bargain sale.' Two days later a lift attendant at a neighbouring shop had his face so badly injured that it was necessary to take him to a hospital. Many cases of scratched faces are reported from many quarters."

The newspapers remind ladies that they are liable to punishment for wounds thus inflicted, and urges them to use guards on the points of their hatpins.

The idea of guards for the points of hatpins is a very good one, but punishment should certainly be inflicted on those who wear these long weapons with exposed points. For "pin-pricks" are becoming more and more serious, and we now frequently find paragraphs referring to trouble with hatpins in any newspaper we happen to take up.

It is difficult, in the absence of Dante, that greatest of experts in the invention of punishments, who, unfortunately, died nearly 600 years ago, to know what to do with these sinners, or what punishment to hold over their heads. But a rift has appeared in this dark

and dangerous cloud, for besides the urgent plea for
guards set forth in the Berlin newspaper, we read in
the *Observer* for Sunday, September 12, 1909, that
M. Lépine, head of the Paris police, ". . . has been
much moved by the number of accidents caused
through the use of ladies' hatpins. Dagger-like points
gleam from out the mass of furs and feathers, to the
infinite danger of other people's eyes. The paternal
Prefect let his wish to curtail this dangerous practice
be known among his protégés, as a stimulus to their
inventiveness. As a consequence, a large part of this
pleasant exhibition (the Lépine Exhibition, held in
the garden of the Tuileries every year for the encouragement of the modest inventors and toymakers
of Paris), of 'camelot' genius, is devoted to women's
hatpins of the safety order."

Besides this, America has also realised that steps
must be taken with regard to hatpins. The Paris
*Daily Mail*, April 18, 1909, says, under the heading
of "Bachelors, Babies, Hatpins, and Baths"—

"According to a New York telegram, a Bill has
been introduced into the Arkansas Legislature It
introduces some most curious laws now under consideration in different States. From Illinois: 'To limit the
length of women's hatpins to nine inches, and make
them take out permits for longer ones, just like all deadly
weapons.'" So it seems that legislation as regards women
and pins is as much required now as in the fifteenth
century B.C. when, as will be remembered, the Athenian
women of the day were deprived of their large pins, in
consequence of the deadly use they made of them.

Let us hope the kind encouragement so thought-
fully given by M. Lépine and the new law from
America will be copied by all nations who wear hat-

I

pins, and thus (though Dante is dead and buried) an end may be put to this most dangerous practice.

The other pin-pricks, the figurative ones, the "coups d'épingle," can, we fear, never be cured. Adam and Eve probably worried each other with them, and all human beings will continue to do so as long as the world exists. Pin-pricks of all kinds are therefore most dangerous things, and when Prévost-Paradol said, "Mille coups d'épingle peuvent donner la fièvre aussi bien qu'une profonde blessure," he helped to confirm this danger. But whether the pricks are most dangerous in a figurative or in a literal sense we cannot say.

Whilst searching for "pin-pricks" in various books, we found in M. Louis De Viel-Castels' *Histoire de la Restauration* that a secret society which existed in France in 1817 formed a conspiracy against the Government of the "Restauration," which conspiracy was called the "Conspiration de l'épingle noire," because the conspirators wore, in some conspicuous place on their persons, a black pin as their sign or token. This adds to the importance of the pin, which is the aim of our work; and so does the expression, "Être tiré à quatre épingles," known to most of our readers, which means, to look very smart, as though just out of a bandbox. Another, not quite so well known, is "Tirer son épingle du jeu," to get out of a scrape, and is explained in a book of French idioms as "Une locution qui vient d'un jeu de petites filles; elles mettent des épingles dans un rond, et avec une balle qui lancée contre le mur, revient vers le rond, elles essayaient d'en faire sortir les épingles: quand on fait sortir la mise, on dit qu'on retire son épingle du jeu." (*French Idioms and Proverbs*, M. de V. Payen-Payne.)

# CHAPTER X

## PINS IN POETRY AND PROSE

" Pricking her fingers with those cursed pins,
Which surely were invented for our sins,—
Making a woman like a porcupine,
Not rashly to be touched."
—BYRON, *Don Juan*, canto VI. stanzas 61, 62.

" SEE a pin and pick it up,
All the day you'll have good luck ;
See a pin and let it lie,
All the day you'll need to cry.

" See a pin and let it lie,
Sure to want before you die ;
See a pin and let it lay,
Will have ill-luck all the day."
—*Well-known rhyme in Worcestershire*

" To see a pin and let it lie,
You'll want a pin before you die."
—W. PENGELLY.

" Needles and pins, needles and pins,
When a man marries his trouble begins."
—*Author unknown.*

" A penny saved is twopence dear ;
A pin a day's a groat a year."
—FRANKLIN, *Hints to those who Would be Rich.*

" See, a pin is there,
A pin a day will fetch a groat a year."
—KING, *Art of Cookery.*

" Not last night, but the night before,
Three great monkeys knocked at my door ;
I jumped up to let them in,
They knocked me down with a tirling-pin."

—*Author Unknown.*


" Pin thy faith to no man's sleeve ; hast thou not
two eyes of thy own ? " —CARLYLE.


In feudal times badges were worn, and the partisans
of a leader used to wear his badge, which was pinned on
the sleeve  Sometimes these badges were changed for
specific purposes, and persons learnt to doubt.  Hence
the phrase, " You wear the badge, but I do not intend to
pin my faith to your sleeve "


" The baker jumped up with surprising agility ;
indeed he managed his pins capitally."

—DE QUINCEY, *Miscellaneous Essays*, " *On
Murder.*"


" He scratched the maid, he stole the cream,
He tore her best lace pinner."

—PRIOR's *Tale of the Widow and her Cat.*


" Now as he scratched to fetch up thought
Forth popped the sprite so thin ;
And from the key-hole bolted out,
All upright as a pin."

—*From* " *Sandy's Ghost,*" *or* " *A Proper
New Ballad in the New Ovid's
Metamorphoses.*"

"And I cleave the black pin in the midst of
the white."

> —MIDDLETON's *No Wit like a Woman's,*
> Act ii. sc. 1.

"Kings are clouts that every man shoots at,
  Our crown the pin that thousands seek to cleave."

> —From " *Tamburlaine the Great.*" *Play
> written by* CHRISTOPHER MARLOWE.

"On the grass an odd dew-drop was glittering yet
  Like aunt's diamond pin on her green tabbinet!"

> —THOMAS MOORE, *The Fudge Family in Paris.*

"One single pin at night let loose
  The robes which veiled her beauty."

> —*From the same.*

"If a toy-shop I step in
  He presents a diamond pin;
  Sweetest token I can wear,
  Which at once may grace my hair."

> —CHRISTOPHER ANSTEY, *New Bath Guide.*

"And first at her porcupine head he begins
  To fumble and poke with irons and pins."

> —*From the same.*

"Here files of pins extend their shining rows,
  Puffs, powders, patches, Bibles, billet-doux."

> —POPE, *The Rape of the Lock.*

" In a translated state then tries the town,
  With borrowed pins and patches not her own."

> —POPE, *Macer: a Character.*

" Chains, coronets, pendans, bracelts, and earings;
  Pins, girdles, spangles, embroideries, and rings;
  Shadoes, rebaltoes, ribbands, ruffs, cuffs, falls,
  Scarfes, feathers, fans, masks, muffs, laces, cauls;
  Thin tiffanies, cobweb lawn, and fardingals,
  Sweet fals, vayles, wimples, glasses, crisping pins;
  Pots of ointment, combes, with poking sticks and
      bodkines,
  Coyfes, gorgets, fringes, rowles, fillets, and hair-laces;
  Silks, damasks, velvet, tinsels, cloth of gold,
  Of tissues with colours of a hundred fold."

> —*" Rhodon and Iris," a play first acted in May,*
> *1631, gives this catalogue of the orna-*
> *ments of a lady of fashion.*

" Pretty maids, pretty pins, pretty women."

> —*One of the " Street Cries of London" about*
> *the beginning of the eighteenth century.*

" The carriage bowls along, and all are pleased
  If Tom be sober, and the wheels well greased;
  But if the rogue have gone a cup too far,
  Left out his linch-pin, or forgot his tar,
  It suffers interruption and delay,
  And meets with hindrance in the smoothest way."

> —COWPER, *The Progress of Errour.*

" A tattered apron hides,
Worn as a cloak, and hardly hides, a gown

More tattered still ; and both but ill conceal
A bosom heaved with never ceasing sighs.
She begs an idle pin of all she meets,
And hoards them in her sleeve ; but needful food,
Tho' pressed with hunger oft, or comelier clothes,
Tho' pinched with cold, asks never—Kate is crazed."

—COWPER, *The Sofa.*

" Their larger minds despise the meaner sins :
They strike with swords, they do not prick with
pins.
Brave to the world, they face home trials ill—
They eat the fruit and blame the woman still "

—D. A. A.

" Let her flaps fly behind her for a yard at the least,
Let her curls meet just under her chin,
Let these curls be supported to keep up the jest,
With an hundred, instead of one pin."

—" *London Magazine,*" *satirising the fashions
of* 1777. *From Chambers's " Book of
Days,*" *vol. ii. page* 47.

" A cap like a hat
(Which was once a cravat)
Part gracefully plaited and pin'd is,
Part struck upon gauze,
Resembles macaws
And all the fine birds of the Indies."

—*The New Bath Guide.*

" A lad when at school, one day stole a pin,
And said that no harm was in such a small sin ;

He next stole a knife, and said 'twas a trifle ;
Next thing he did was pockets to rifle ;
Next thing he did was a house to break in ;
The next thing—upon a gallows to swing.
So let us avoid all little sinnings,
Since such is the end of petty beginnings."

>—" *The Ranks in Life : for the Amusement and
> Instruction of Youth,*" *J. Drury.    From
> "Forgotten  Children's  Books,"  brought
> together  by  Mr.  Andrew  W.  Tuer,
> F.S.A.*

" *Miss and Her Pin.*"
" My Knot and my Hood,
   It sticks in the Mode,
My Kercher in Order it places ;
It fixes my Ruffles
And other Pantoffles,
In their Plaits it keeps all my Laces."

>—"*Songs for Little Misses," from "Puerilia ;
> or, Amusements  for  the  Young,*" *by
> John Marchant, Gent.   London : P.
> Stevens, 1751.*

"Some pitch their tent-pole, and pin down the lines
   That stretch the o'er-awning canvas."

>                    —SOUTHEY.

" Pin a dish-clout to his tail."
>    —SWIFT, *May's Letters to Dr. Sheridan.*

### The Argument.

". . . Sin and death . . . resolve to sit no longer
confined in hell, but to follow Satan their sire  up to

the place of man: to make the way easier from hell
to this world to and fro, they pave a broad highway,
or bridge, over Chaos, (and)

> ". . . with pins of adamant
>   and chains they made all fast—"

—MILTON, *Paradise Lost.* Book X.

> " Why, I dared not name a sin
>   In her presence : I went round,
>   Clipped its name and shut it in
>   Some mysterious crystal sound—
>   Changed the dagger for the pin."

—ELIZABETH BARRETT BROWNING,
  " *Where's Agnes ?* "

> "Oh cousin, let us be content, in work
>   To do the thing we can, and not presume
>   To fret because it's little.   'Twill employ
>   Seven men, they say, to make a perfect pin ;
>   Who makes the head, content to miss the point,
>   Who makes the point, agreed to leave the join :
>   And if a man should cry, 'I want a pin,
>   And I must make it straightway, head and point,'
>   His wisdom is not worth the pin he wants.
>   Seven men to a pin—and not a man too much ! "

—E. B. BROWNING, *Aurora Leigh.* Book VIII.

> "I do not set my life at a pin's fee."

—*Hamlet*   Act. i. sc. 4.

> "Then will she get the upshot by cleaving the pin."

—*Love's Labour's Lost.*   Act iv. sc. 1.

" I would not care a pin, if the other three were in."

—Ibid.   Act iv. sc. 3.

" And Nestor play at push-pin with the boys."

—Ibid.   Act iv. sc. 3.

" This gallant pins the wenches on his sleeve."

—Ibid.   Act v. sc. 2.

" . . . and all eyes blind
With the pin and web."

—Winter's Tale.   Act i. sc. 2.

" Pins and poking-sticks of steel,
What maids lack from head to heel."

—Ibid.   Act iv. sc. 4.

" . . . she lifted the princess from the earth, and so locks her in embracing, as if she would pin her to her heart."

—Ibid.   Act v. sc. 2.

" Strike in their numb'd and mortified bare arms
Pins, wooden pricks."

—King Lear.   Act ii. sc. 3.

" . . . he gives the web and the pin " (meaning a malady of the eye).

—Ibid.   Act iii. sc. 4.

" Comes at the last, and with a little pin
Bores through his castle-wall, and—farewell,
King ! "

—Richard II.   Act iii. sc. 2.

" My wretchedness unto a row of pins,
They'll talk of state."

*—Ibid.* Act iii. sc. 4.

". . . the very
Pin of his heart " (*i.e.* the centre).

*—Romeo and Juliet.* Act ii. sc. 4.

". . . come, tell a pin : you are foresworn."

*—Troilus and Cressida* Act v. sc. 2.

". . . with hearts in their bellies no bigger than pins' heads."

*—Henry IV.* Part I. Act iv. sc. 2.

" Die men like dogs! give crowns like pins!"

*—Henry IV.* Part II. Act ii. sc 4.

". . . for his apparel is built upon his back, and the whole frame stands upon pins."

*—Henry IV.* Part II. Act iii. sc. 2.

". . . which show like pins' heads to her."

*—Henry IV.* Part II. Act iv. sc. 3.

". . . but I'll make thee eat iron like an ostrich, and swallow my sword like a great pin, ere thou and I part."

*—Henry VI.* Part II. Act iv. sc. 10.

". . . the kitchen maulkin pins
Her richest lockram 'bout her reechy neck."

*—Coriolanus.* Act ii. sc. 1.

" From a pound to a pin ? "
*— Two Gentlemen of Verona.* Act. i. sc. 1.

"A round hose, madam, now's not worth a pin."
—*Two Gentlemen of Verona.*    Act ii. sc. 7.

"Tut, a pin! this shall be answered."
—*Merry Wives of Windsor.*    Act. i. sc. 1.

"No matter for the dish, sir.    No indeed, sir, not of a pin."
—*Measure for Measure.*    Act ii. sc. 1.

". . . if you should need a pin,
You could not with more tame a tongue desire it."
—*Measure for Measure.*    Act ii. sc. 2.

"O, were it but my life, I'd throw it down for your
        deliverance,
As frankly as a pin."
—*Measure for Measure.*    Act iii. sc. 1.

"A rush, a hair, a drop of blood, a pin, a nut, a cherry stone."
—*Comedy of Errors.*    Act iv. sc. 3.

"Scratch thee but with a pin, and there remains some scar of it."
—*As You Like It.*    Act iii. sc. 5.

"Begin with needles and prines, and leave off with horse and horn'd nout."

"Scotch proverb intimating that 'they who begin with pilfering and picking, will not stop there, but proceed to greater crimes'"—KELLY.

"For spleen indulged will banish rest,
Far frae the bosoms of the best;
Thousands a year's no worth a prin,
Whene'er this fashious guest gets in."

—ALLAN RAMSAY.

"Prin up your aprons baith, and come away."

—*From the same.*

"No worth a prein-head."

—*Author Unknown.*

"My memory's no worth a preen;
I had amaist forgotten clean."

—*Postscript to a letter written by Robert Burns.*

"Donald Din,
Built his house without a pin."

—*An Ayrshire rhyme, probably very old.*

"There stands a castle in the west,
They ca' it Donald Din;
There's no a nail in a' its roof,
Nor yet a wooden pin."

*The Historie and Dessent of the House of Rowallane.*
". . . alluding to Dundonald Castle, the ancient seat of
King Robert II, and now the last remaining property in
Ayrshire of the noble family who take their title from it
According to tradition, it was built by a hero, Donald Din,
or Din Donald, and constructed entirely of stone, without
the use of wood. It is situated in Kyle-Stewart."

—R. CHAMBERS, *Popular Rhymes of Scotland.*

"Kate, wa'n't I such a one as he?
As like him, ay, as pin to pin."
—R. BLOOMFIELD, *Richard and Kate.*


"But, thought I, it is hard if I cannot stalk you,
that have stalked so many bucks.   If so, I had better
give my shafts to be pudding pins."
—SIR WALTER SCOTT, *Peveril of the Peak.*
Vol. i. p. 205.


"Mistress Deborah kept Julian waiting till she
had prinked herself and pinned herself."
—*Ibid.*   Vol. i. p. 270.


"I will not ride that great Holstein brute, that
I must climb up to by a ladder, and then sit like a
pincushion on an elephant."
—*Ibid.*   Vol. ii p. 268.


"After Mason has been attacked by the maniac
(Mrs. Rochester, his sister), and wounded by her, he
says to Rochester, 'She's done for me, I fear,' and
Rochester replies, 'Not a whit! courage! This day
fortnight you'll hardly be a pin the worse of it.'"
—CHARLOTTE BRONTE, *Jane Eyre.*


"But old Benjy was young Master's real delight
and refuge. . . . A cheery, humorous, kind-hearted
old man, full of sixty years of Vale gossip, and of
all sorts of helpful ways for young and old, but
above all for children.   It was he who bent the first
pin with which Tom extracted his first stickleback

out of 'Pebbly Brook,' the little stream which ran through the village."

—T. Hughes, *Tom Brown's Schooldays.*

"Lizzie took wee Jeannie on her knee, and proceeded to make the child as neat as a new pin."

—J. J. B., *Wee Macgreegor.*

"John's collar came loose, and the stud broke just at the critical moment when the photographer was about to take a family group. Lizzie looked up quickly, and whipped something from near her waist. 'John,' she said, 'gang to the ither room, an' see if I left my caim on the table.' Her voice sank to a whisper, 'an'—an'—here twa preens.'"

—*From the same.*

"The widow Broddy by the slap,
 Wha sold the tartan preen-cods,
 By whisky maul'd, lay but her cap,
 Her head upon a green sod,
   Right sick that day."

—Davidson's *Seasons, &c.,* p. 78.

# CHAPTER XI

## THE PIN IN PLACE-NAMES—HAIRPIN CORNERS —PIN-CURLS—WEDDING CUSTOMS—FUNERAL CUSTOMS

" A pin-drop silence strikes o'er all the place "
—LEIGH HUNT, *Rimini*, i. 244 (1816)

THE history of ancient and modern pins is indeed inexhaustible, and, like Tennyson's song of "The Brook," it might "go on for ever," for there are still many things we should wish to say about them. We will, however, confine ourselves to a few odds and ends, which have no particular place anywhere, yet cannot be left out, for they help to fill the niches and corners of our subject, just as those little Alpine plants, beloved of gardeners, fill the niches of a rock garden. First, we will beg the superstitious to remember, if they truly love and value their pins and their friends, that when offering one to a friend it should be handed head first, as sharp and pointed things cut love; this is very important. And, by-the-by, though what follows has nothing whatever to do with pins, useful information is always acceptable, and it would be unkind not to remind the superstitious that they must never tell their dreams fasting, and must always tell them first to a woman called Mary. Those who want money will be glad to know that if, by accident, they find the back tooth of a horse and carry it about with them as long as they live, they will *never* want money; but the tooth must be found by chance.

We should perhaps mention the fact that pins, whatever they were in ancient times, are now more essentially of feminine use. It is true men wear scarf-pins and tie-pins; these came into fashion a very long time ago, and a beautiful specimen of a gold and coral double pin connected by a gold chain and worn by John Frederick Sackville, third Duke of Dorset, is shewn in Illustration 2 (Plate X.). Some early portraits of Charles Dickens also exhibit two pins connected by a chain in his cravat, following the type of those used in the Bronze Age, of which we also give an illustration (Plates III. and IV). Jewelled pins are still given by royal personages to officials as acknowledgment of service rendered.

In some parts of England, about forty years ago, the dame of a school used to obtain silence in this way: she held up a pin and said, " I want to hear this pin drop." Her scholars listened and heard the pin drop upon the brick floor; she would then proceed with what she had to tell them.

Many of our readers are no doubt aware that at Monte Carlo those who play the game of " trente et quarante " are given a pin and a little card, upon which, with pricks, they keep count of their winnings and losses.

It is not perhaps generally known that pins are very little used by the Chinese, strings, knots, and loops taking their place. Pin is also a term of Chinese diplomacy, signifying a petition or address from foreigners to the Emperor of China or any of his viceroys or deputies.

Motorists, especially racers, must be well acquainted

with those dangerous bends in roads called "hairpin corners." There is a good example of these bends in the Elan Valley, North Wales, and another near Ramsey in the Isle of Man.

We could give a long list of places with pin-names. In London we have Pinner's Alley in Shoreditch, Pin Alley, near Rosemary Lane, and Pinner's Court, Old Broad Street, where was originally Pinner's Hall, and where no pin-maker's foot-fall has been heard for many a long year. There is Pinner's Green in Essex; Pin-hoe, near Exeter · a brook called the "Pin" runs through this parish, and Pin-hoe is generally understood to mean "the height of the pin." At Pinner in Middlesex there is also a Pin brook, but why these brooks were given the name, unless on account of their being very small, no one seems to know.

A "pinner" is a woman's head-dress, and it also meant (anciently) a pounder of cattle, a man who puts cattle into a pound, a pound-keeper.

Pinner was also an apron covering the front of the dress, formerly pinned on, now called a pinafore.

It is possible that one of these may have had something to do with calling these places "Pinner." But the interpretation of place-names is a separate and most interesting study, which is not dealt with in this book.

Some of these names are, however, quite easy to interpret. Pin Oak, U.S.A., for instance, must be named after a species of oak called pin-oak, which is found in North America. This oak is so called from its persistent dead branches, which resemble pins fixed on the trunk.

Pinnock (Cornwall) would be named after the hedge-sparrow pin-ok.

The pieces used for a game of chess used to be called chess-pins. "The king is the first and highest of all the chesse pins." (R. Holme, *The Academy of Armoury*, vol. ii. book iii. chap. 16.

A periwinkle is called a "pin-patch" because it is extracted from its shell with a pin.

Pin-spotted materials have a number of small spots like pin-heads forming a pattern on them.

Pin-striped materials have a very narrow line or stripe of the thickness of a pin.

Pin-tucks are the smallest made and no wider than a pin.

A pin-horse is the middle one of a team of three horses.

"Pins and needles" is a feeling of pricking under the skin: "on pins and needles," in a state of excessive uneasiness. "He had enough pins and needles in his feet to stock a haberdasher's shop." (Routledge's *Every Boy's Annual*, 640.)

"On one's pins" means on one's legs, in good condition.

Pin-ball sight is a small bead sight.

To "under-pin" is to insert masonry beneath a portion of wall that needs support.

All our cooks use pudding-pins, and we must not forget that knitting-needles are sometimes called "pins." "As the old lady put down her pins, the princess took them up, and finished the stocking heel." (*Tit-Bits*, 4th December 1897.)

And quoting from "The Horkey," a Suffolk ballad, by Robert Bloomfield, we find knitting-pins again :—

"Ah ! Judie Twicket ! though thou'rt dead,
        With thee the tale begins ;
For still seems thrumming in my head
        The rattling of thy pins.
Poor Judie !  Thus Time knits or spins
        The worsted from Life's ball !
Death stopt thy tales, and stopt thy pins,
        And so he'll serve us all."

Horkey is the Suffolk name for " harvest home." Judie Twicket was a real person who, whilst she knitted, related tales of the harvest home and other things.

There are pins in musical instruments.

Many ladies wear pin-curls, a little useful bunch of curls fastened to a hairpin, which can be bought for a few shillings. "She buys a 'pin-curl' and fastens it to her cycling hat."

*The Two Pins* was the name of a play produced at the Aldwych Theatre not long ago  At the same theatre, *Pins, Feathers, and the Lady Elsa* ran for a short time ; this was followed by *The Pin and the Pudding.*

It is quite true that once upon a time, about sixty years ago perhaps, some Irish ladies of " high degree " used thorns for keeping their clothes together, and for various other purposes, to save buying pins, thus reverting to the original of all pins.  They were not poor, but were looked upon as misers, and we think their mental condition must have been peculiar.

The Irish for pin is " bioran," pronounced bir-aun. In Scotland it is " prein."  The smallest of pins is called a " minikin prein," whilst the largest is denominated a " bodle prein."  Minikin is anything that is small.  In Welsh a pin is just a " pin," as in English.

In the north of Scotland there is a superstition that all the pins which have been used in dressing a bride on her marriage day must be thrown away, as it would be unlucky to use them again.

It was once the custom at Irish weddings for the bride to have two ribbons pinned in a cross at the back of her dress before going to church, and if she came back without them it was thought a good omen for her happiness. The bride's mother gave her a shilling before going to church, and the bridegroom's father gave him a five-shilling piece. These they hid in the stones on the hearth in their bedroom with a harrow-pin, thus burying their bad luck  A harrow is an agricultural implement set with a row of iron points called pins.

And now it would seem our work is drawing to its close, for we must bring to the notice of our readers those final scenes connected with the end of human life which it is fitting should be kept to the last, and which appear also to have their peculiar significance.

In some parts of England there is still a prevailing idea that carrying a corpse across private property constitutes a right of way. A village undertaker once asked a tenant farmer during a flood to allow a corpse to be carried across his field to the church-yard. The farmer hesitated, for the reason above mentioned. But the undertaker promised to stick six black pins in the gate-posts of the fields through which the funeral would pass, and in this way the path remained private. Undoubtedly the pins were a fee and acknowledgment that permission was given as a favour for that occasion only.

The pins employed for any purpose on a corpse

are never used again, but are always deposited in the coffin and buried with the dead.

Therefore we feel the time has come to end this history of the " pin." We have followed its checkered career through many vicissitudes, and it has been our earnest endeavour throughout to verify all that has been said ; but, to use the words of Mr. Andrew Lang in his *Magic and Religion*, the " perhapses," the " we may supposes," and the " we must infers ' are countless.

But what more can we say to the glory of the pin? Have we proved that it is not the insignificant thing many suppose it to be—that there is hardly anything more valuable, nothing we make more constant use of, nothing we should miss more were pins to become extinct, and nothing to which we give less thought? We have proved it to be one of the oldest things in the world ; it is of interest to the most learned and scientific scholars, and there is not a human being, young or old, rich or poor, who does not know what a pin is. It cannot be dispensed with at the beginning of life ; is one of the first things required when a child is born into the world ; it is also used at every burial, and it would be impossible even to imagine the many millions of times a pin is used between birth and death. Without it, existence would be very difficult ; in fact, almost impossible, at any rate to women ; we do not think that is saying too much. There is, however, one thing about them of which, with the deepest regret, we must confess to know nothing, one secret they hold which we cannot guess, one question that no one in the whole world can answer. And you, dear reader, who have followed us thus far so patiently, listen whilst we whisper it in your

ear, " Where do all the lost pins go to ? "—the millions
and millions of pins that disappear each day and hour
and minute of our lives from the humblest cottages
and the most magnificent palaces. They vanish, we
know not how, we know not whither, and all the
cleverest and most curious people in the world have
never yet been able to discover what becomes of them.
It was said more than fifty years ago that if pins
continued to be lost as they were then, some day or
other the whole world would be found to be one vast
mass of pins. That day has not yet arrived, and as
pins continue to vanish in larger quantities than ever,
we must look for some other solution of their ulti-
mate fate. M'Donald Clarke gives us a rather charming
idea in some lines which thus describe the closing
day—

> " Now twilight lets her curtain down,
> And pins it with a star "

Is there, then, perhaps a paradise for pins, into which
they pass when lost or mislaid, and where they are
transformed into stars? A great number would be
necessary to pin down twilight's curtain, and when

> " . . . one more day
> Drops in the shadowy gulf of bygone things "

many more would be required to fasten the darker
and deeper one of night.

Still the question is unanswered, still the mystery
of lost pins remains; it is therefore with reluctance
we leave the subject, for our task is but imperfectly
performed. We have, however, proved the ancient
origin of the pin, and traced its glorious history to
the best of our ability from the original thorn which

fastened the skin coverings of our prehistoric fore-fathers, and was followed by the pins made of bone, bronze, gold, silver, brass, and iron, to the present modern steel pin. If we have also touched it with the spirit of romance, and crowned it with greater importance, then our labour will not have been in vain.

# CHAPTER XII

## PINCUSHIONS

"Thou art a retailer of Phrases, and dost deal in Remnants of Remnants, like a maker of Pincushions"—CONGREVE'S *Way of the World*

WE must now turn our thoughts to the various ways which have existed at different times for keeping or storing pins. It is "a far cry" from the days when those ladies who dwelt in caves and gathered thorns, or made pins from the fibulæ of animals with which to fasten their clothing, to the present time when hardly any room is thought completely furnished without a pincushion of some kind at hand, well stocked with all kinds of pins. The wardrobe of ladies in those early days was no doubt very limited, and probably the pins were seldom removed, but if any emergency arose to oblige their doing so, the floor of the cave would surely have made as good a pincushion as the occasion demanded. Many hundreds of years must have passed away before any real way of storing pins was dreamt of, and even at the present day in some parts of the world where thorns are still used as pins, there is most likely no way of keeping them except stuck in the dress itself. That this way of keeping pins still exists, we all know, especially those who employ a certain class of dressmaker called always a "clever little woman," though sometimes six feet high and two yards round the waist ! The "little woman" also stores pins in her

153

mouth, which reminds us of Miss Edgeworth's tale of a governess, looked upon by her pupils as the essence of politeness and elegance, until one day in an unguarded moment when arranging her pupil's sash she put several pins into her mouth, thus revealing her origin as a dressmaker, for *no* other woman in those days of ultra-refinement ever did this. But we are digressing.

We have said that many hundreds of years passed away before any real way of storing pins was even dreamt of; many more must have passed before they began to take even the shadow of their present place in society, and it took a still longer period to make them inexpensive and plentiful. It was therefore first of all their great value that made it necessary to preserve them so carefully. An interesting article by Mrs. Head on "Some Old-fashioned Pincushions," which appeared in the *Queen* of March 7, 1903, throws some light on this point, and says: ". . . in those early days when pins of metal were costly and much-prized possessions, they were doubtless kept in some less insecure receptacle than an uncovered pincushion, and therefore the pin-box is probably a far less recent invention than the pincushion." Mrs. Head's idea must be correct, and many of the silver boxes of ancient date that now stand amongst a host of other articles on a table set apart for them in our drawing-rooms, may very likely have begun life as pin-boxes. We also find at a later date that our grandmothers carried in their pockets small metal or wooden cases called pin-poppets, which, though not exactly boxes, had lids and were both safe and convenient. They held needles as well as pins, but were invariably called *pin*-poppets. The metal one

PLATE XXV

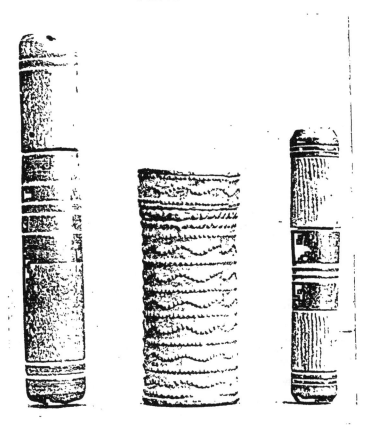

Wooden Pin poppet
*Actual size*

1 Metal Pin-poppet
*Actual size*

3 Wooden Pin poppet
*Actual size*

4 Ivory Pin box
*Actual size*

(Plate XXV., Illustration 1) is embossed all round, and has a hinged lid; the workmanship, though somewhat rude, has a certain quaint beauty of its own. Those of wood are in two parts, which fit together, as is plainly shewn in Plate XXV., Illustrations 2 and 3.

The little ivory box (Plate XXV., Illustration 4) is of a later date, and holds only a few pins. It is impossible to speak with any certainty of the age of the pin-poppets; they may have been in use long before our grandmothers' time, and we may reasonably suppose that boxes or cases of some kind in metal or wood were employed for keeping pins before the reign of Queen Elizabeth (this being the date of the earliest pincushion we illustrate), for are we not told that in 1347, 12,000 pins were delivered from the royal wardrobe for the use of Princess Joan of France? and it will be remembered that in Chapter I., referring to the household accounts of Katherine, Countess of Devon, in 1524, a "pin-case, 16d." is mentioned amongst other "necessaries for my lady."

It is however, very difficult to trace the origin of pincushions, and a woman's bodice was no doubt one of its earliest and favourite forms, for this convenient way of keeping pins probably existed in very primitive times. Pillows and cushions are also frequently mentioned in the Bible, and perhaps pincushions may have had their origin in the pillow, made smaller; although the idea of doing this, and adapting the smaller pillow or cushion for pins, may not have occurred to any one till pins became plentiful and were made in small sizes

In confirmation of this we find that in the sixteenth and seventeenth centuries pincushions were called pin-pillows—"pyn-pyllows to stycke pynnes on," 1588;

"pinpillowe's of cloth for children" in 1622. And in 1650 we hear that "they of S. Christopher's stick pins on their noses, making their noses serve for pin-pillows"! The inhabitants of S. Christopher were no doubt singular in many of their customs, and this way of keeping pins is certainly unique; handy perhaps, but painful, and very awkward with a cold in the head.

We have already said that our search for pin-cushions takes us back to the reign of Queen Elizabeth; these early pincushions were of course treated with much respect and consideration, for they were of great value, not only because of the pins they held, but on account of the exquisite needlework with which they were adorned. In many of them the work is faded and worn, but enough remains to test its original excellence, and here and there we find one of exceptional beauty—a picture indeed, painted in silks with a needle. They were all of them too big for the pocket, so doubtless the pin-poppets were carried about long after pincushions were made, whilst the pin-cushions themselves may have spent much of their time in strict retirement, carefully preserved under lock and key, to be brought out only on special occasions when some elaborate toilet of their owner's required the pins they held. It is quite likely that only a few precious or jewelled pins were kept in these larger and more elaborately worked pincushions, and this may explain the absence of pin marks in many of them. There seems to have been no great change in the shape of pincushions for nearly 200 years after the reign of Elizabeth. They were till then, with a few exceptions, square or oblong, thick or thin, according to taste; some had tassels at each corner, and some an edging of silver lace or cord. Great variety was, however, shewn in the work of their decoration, which combined great beauty of execution with richness and variety of colour and design.

In the late part of the seventeenth century we find a round pincushion for suspension from the girdle covered with silver thread and mounted in silver, which is a great change from the old form, and another decorated with pins instead of needlework is dated 1652.

Knitted pincushions, mostly round, came in about the middle of the eighteenth century, but the spirit of caprice did not really touch these articles till the beginning of the nineteenth century, and from then till now has pursued its fantastic progress until there is scarcely anything a pincushion has not been made to represent.

Some of these old pincushions were stuffed with waste bits of rag; small pieces of flannel have also been much used, and are still used occasionally; others were filled with sand. The heavy pincushions were used for pinning work to, work which had to be stretched while it was done, otherwise ladies pinned their work to their knees. We might just as well inform our readers that "Queen Anne is dead" as tell them that pincushions are now usually stuffed with bran, and yet their history can hardly be complete without some mention of that most valuable commodity. Mrs. Head, in the article to which we have already referred, goes on to say that ". . the cult of the pincushion, if I may call it so, certainly reached its zenith in early Victorian days, when bazaars first came into vogue, bazaars whereat every stall was devoted to 'fancy work,' and every bit of this 'fancy work' was made at home. Under such conditions

it was natural that the pincushion—easy to manufacture out of the merest scraps, pretty to look at,
and not absolutely useless—always occupied a conspicuous place among the stock of dainty trifles, and
so our grandmothers came to develop a perfect genius
for making it in every possible form.   They contrived
the tiniest of cushions for the pocket, the smartest of
box-cushions for the dressing-table, the biggest and
most commodious for the workroom ; and even the
kitchen was supplied with one, a favourite type for
the latter situation being a gigantic heart or diamond,
covered with blue or purple merino, or with multi-
coloured patchwork, and edged with a ruche of scarlet
braid."   This covers a considerable amount of ground
concerning pincushions of that period when the bazaar
or fancy fair began to wield its fatal spell over the
world in general.   That it still continues to do so we
all know to our cost.   Perhaps some of our readers
may have come across a charmingly old-fashioned
book called *Treasures of Needlework*, published about
1860, but for the benefit of those who have not had
this privilege, we give here its full title and dedication.

"*Treasures of Needlework*.   By Mrs. Warren and
Mrs. Pullen, illustrated with useful and ornamental
designs, patterns, &c.   To Lady Needleworkers
throughout the world this Book is dedicated by
the Authors, in the hope that it may aid in the pro-
duction of those Ornamental and Useful Articles that
add Elegance to the Boudoir, and Yield Profit to the
Fancy Fair."

Could anything be more exquisitely refined?   It
makes one long to dip into this volume, and we
will do so without delay.   A "pendant pincushion
in application" is thus described: "This toilet-

cushion is in a style which is new, even on the Continent, and has never yet been introduced into this country." Another "toilet-cushion" (designed by Mrs. Warren) is said to be in crochet entirely, and the word "*pins*" is cleverly and elegantly worked into the centre; it is oblong shaped. Mrs. Pullen describes another pincushion which is also decorated with crochet, and there is a beautiful picture of it in the book. It is round, and in the centre is a round hole into which is placed what Mrs. Pullen calls a "handsome toilet-bottle," though she adds, "a small vase of flowers looks equally well." We can some of us remember a toilet-cushion of this kind in the best spare bedrooms of our maiden aunts or old-fashioned friends, and how we gazed with almost sacred awe upon that central vase of flowers, wondering in our youthful hearts what kind of guest could be thought worthy of so exquisite a toilet-cushion.

A few years ago we remember that a friend had a stall at a bazaar in the country, which consisted of pincushions entirely. Many months were spent in making and collecting everything that imagination could devise or fertile brains conceive in the way of pincushions. Mrs. Warren's and Mrs. Pullen's "treasures" would have been an invaluable assistance on this occasion, but unfortunately at that time we were not acquainted with these ladies or their book. If all the pincushions set out on this stall were sold, each house in that country town where the bazaar was held must still be well stocked with them. Some were very curious, and we remember one in particular which was much observed and talked of. It was sent from the East End of London (we think it was made by a cabman, or perhaps his wife). It was beautiful to behold, and much decorated with beads; there were two, or perhaps three pins in it, but not more. The reason of this was soon discovered. The pins could only be put in with a hammer, and it was quite impossible to take them out except with a pair of pincers! Heaven only knows what it was stuffed with, probably bits of old cabs. We believe that it found its way into a local museum, with a hammer and a pair of pincers, and a charge of one penny made for putting in a pin or taking one out. We do not recollect ever to have heard of a quite similar pincushion " even on the Continent," but a great many are now made merely to attract the eye, and though not stuffed with wood, the pincushion itself is often of the poorest, and seemingly the last thing thought of. Every imaginable thing is represented, and towards Christmas the shops seem to vie with each other in making pincushions of the most grotesque and unsuitable forms But people's tastes vary, and the public must be pleased. What one person considers frightful will be treasured as a work of art by another, and who can say which has the better taste. One thing is certain, the pincushion is far too valuable an article ever to go out of fashion. We may have to endure it in the shape of an airship flapping about our rooms, or in some other form equally unpleasant and unsuitable, but have it we must; the cry for a pin, at any and every hour of the day or night, is one that must be answered. The pincushion is indispensable. Small wonder, then, that new forms are constantly invented, the demand being so great. We quite recognise the necessity and charm of novelty, but those who wish to escape from a too advanced form in pincushions must turn back into the past and copy the old ones.

Then we shall find something upon which our eyes can rest with pleasure, and learn that even a pincushion may be "a thing of beauty and a joy for ever."

Many beautiful pincushions are still made, but the most beautiful always take the simple form of those used in olden days But though simple in form they are often elaborately decorated with graceful designs in needlework, and the effect is one of great beauty. As a rule they have been carefully and kindly dealt with, but we sometimes find the materials of which they are constructed fast wearing out, and in many the colours have long ago faded into shades so delicate it would be impossible to describe. But if the touch of a magic wand could restore them to their pristine brilliance and at the same time give some of these old pincushions the gift of speech, what interesting and romantic tales might be unfolded to us—tales that would carry us back into that golden age we call the " past," over which it is so customary to mourn. Then, perhaps, when the day is over and the night of pleasure about to begin, we might close our eyes and see in a vision some dainty maiden at her toilet, pausing a moment to enjoy the happy dreams of anticipation, the while she toys with the pins upon her cushion. Each pin is listening to the beatings of her heart, and learning all its secrets from the little sighs, the smiles, and perhaps the tears that are dropped upon it. Each one hopes to be chosen to fasten her only ornament, a deep red rose, to the bosom of her dress, and to rest there for all that happy evening. And then, when at last the maiden returns flushed and tired from the dance, the pin, safe back in the cushion, will tell the other pins how the evening has been spent, and of

L

the gallant youth who was ever at the maiden's side. And sometimes when, her features touched by some transfiguring fire, the maiden's thoughts are too far off to be disturbed, the pins chatter quite loud— for pins—and that perhaps is how the pincushions learn all about their owners, and why they are so interesting.

Let us now turn Plate XXVI, which is called " A pincushion of Elizabeth " The work is exquisite, representing in long and short stitches the woman of Samaria in the centre, and David playing upon the harp at the top on the right. We wish it were possible to tell our readers what vanished hands traced these figures, and the flowers, birds, and insects which also appear upon this pincushion. Queen Elizabeth herself excelled in needlework; it was one of the resources with which she whiled away many weary hours of her imprisonment at Woodstock, and history relates that at the age of six she presented her brother Edward with a shirt of cambric of her own work. Luxurious, vain, and pleasure-loving, she had an inordinate love of dress, jewels, and every kind of finery, and was much displeased if the ladies of her court wore dresses finer than her own. She would be sure to have had a beautiful pincushion, and if this one is not her handiwork it may well have been one of her cherished possessions, and then what tales of this great queen a romantic pin could weave!

Queen Elizabeth had an ungovernable and overbearing temper, and is said to have boxed the ears of her favourites and to have sworn at her ministers " like a fish-wife," but she worked hard for the good of her country, and had much sympathy with her people;

PLATE XXVI

Pincushion of the time of Queen Elizabeth. (Size, 9¾ in. × 6 in.)

and if sometimes unhappy memories filled her heart with remorse, and the floodgates of her confidence were only opened in the privacy of her own apartment with the silence of the night around her, the pins upon her cushion can alone have heard them. They alone can have seen this queen with the barriers of her great position swept away, revealing a woman who, though emotionally cold, had learnt from the severe teaching of experience that love, trust, and confidence are all beset with dangers, and that a queen, however great, must stand alone. The pins, erect upon the royal cushion, watched and listened, we may be sure; and afterwards, how they must have talked! and to some purpose, especially a few that perhaps got lost, and, wandering into the pincushions of writers of history, there continued to discourse. How otherwise could we possibly know so much about "Good Queen Bess."

Plate XXVII., Illustration 1, though of the same period, is in striking contrast to Plate XXVI. The simplicity of the design, which repeats itself in graceful curves, is very restful to the eye; and though worked on linen, threads of silver and an edging of serrated silver thread lace give to it, even after the lapse of years, a bright and gay appearance. The design consists of continuous scrolling stems bearing leaves, flowers (including columbines, pinks, &c ), and fruits (strawberries, peas, acorns, &c ). On each strawberry a bee is perched. The stems are worked in looped gilt thread stitched down with green; the flowers, fruit, and leaves with silver and silver-gilt thread worked over with bright colours. Parts of the cushion are not worked, or are only outlined, and the design can be seen drawn

on the linen. These are the only two pincushions
we have found belonging to the sixteenth century.
In the seventeenth century we begin with a Jacobean
pincushion (Plate XXVII., Illustration 2), covered
with canvas, embroidered with coloured silks chiefly
in tent and cross stitches, and with silver thread in
short and chain stitches; panels of various devices
appear on each side of the cushion, in the manner of
samplers—in one panel is a lady with a ruff, and high
puffed sleeves, hooped skirt, and a feather fan; in other
panels we find lions and unicorns, roses, fleur-de-lys;
clasped hands with olive branches, animals, love-
knots; and the letters I and R (James Rex) royally
crowned.

Illustration 3, Plate XXVII., has the marks of pins
on both sides, but the pins themselves seem to have
joined that invisible army of lost pins which is one of
the puzzles of the world. This pincushion is oblong,
and one side of it is embroidered in diamond diaper
stitch, in various colours; the reverse side has bands of
chevron ornamentation in the same colours. There are
tassels at each corner.

Illustration 4 on the same plate contains treasures
that have been well guarded by succeeding generations
of owners. The bag and pincushion are of canvas, embroidered in coloured silks and silver-gilt thread on a
silver thread ground. The bag has a flowering tree on
each side, and the pincushion has a symmetrical floral
device. The two are united by a cord of plaited silk
with tassels, and were apparently worn round the waist
in the fashion of a girdle. Imagination supplies a
list of interesting articles that may at different times
have rested in the dainty little bag—fans, scents,
pomades, and *billet-doux* no doubt, and later on between

on the linen. These are the only two pincushions we have found belonging to the sixteenth century. In the seventeenth century we begin with a Jacobean pincushion (Plate XXVII., Illustration 2), covered with canvas, embroidered with coloured silks chiefly in tent and cross stitches, and with silver thread in short and chain stitches; panels of various devices appear on each side of the cushion, in the manner of samplers—in one panel is a lady with a ruff, and high puffed sleeves, hooped skirt, and a feather fan; in other panels we find lions and unicorns, roses, fleur-de-lys; clasped hands with olive branches, animals, love-knots; and the letters I and R (James Rex) royally crowned.

Illustration 3, Plate XXVII., has the marks of pins on both sides, but the pins themselves seem to have joined that invisible army of lost pins which is one of the puzzles of the world. This pincushion is oblong, and one side of it is embroidered in diamond diaper stitch, in various colours; the reverse side has bands of chevron ornamentation in the same colours. There are tassels at each corner.

Illustration 4 on the same plate contains treasures that have been well guarded by succeeding generations of owners. The bag and pincushion are of canvas, embroidered in coloured silks and silver-gilt thread on a silver thread ground. The bag has a flowering tree on each side, and the pincushion has a symmetrical floral device. The two are united by a cord of plaited silk with tassels, and were apparently worn round the waist in the fashion of a girdle. Imagination supplies a list of interesting articles that may at different times have rested in the dainty little bag—fans, scents, pomades, and *billet-doux* no doubt, and later on between

PLATE XXVII

1 Pincushion of the time of Queen Elizabeth

(Size, 9 in × 6 in)

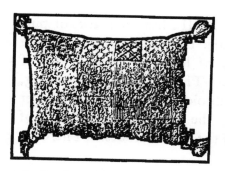

2 Jacobean Pincushion    (Size, 11 in × 8 in)

4 Bag and Pincushion of Canvas
(English)

(Size, 2 in × 2 in)

17th century

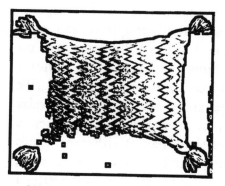

3 Oblong Pincushion of Canvas    (English)

(Size, 6½ in × 5½ in)

17th century

PLATE XXVIII

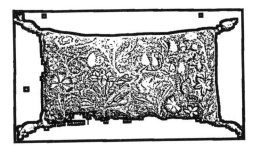

1. Canvas Pincushion embroidered in Coloured Silks.
(English.   Size, 10 in. × 5¾ in.)
*17th century.*

2. Pincushion decorated with Pins, with date 1652.
(English.   Size, 13 in. × 9½ in.)

3. Spangled Pincushion from Knole.
(Size, 11 in. × 7¼ in.)

them the bag and cushion may perhaps have held some of

"The powders, patches, and the pins,
The ribbons, jewels, and the rings,
The lace, the paint, and warlike things,
That made up all their magazines"

—COWLEY.

Wonderful needlework is displayed in Plate XXVIII., Illustration 1, a canvas pincushion embroidered in coloured silk on a silver thread ground. Each flower is perfect. here is the rose, the thistle, and the lily, and the old-fashioned pink, whilst the caterpillar and the snail are cleverly introduced, as well as that most attractive little animal the squirrel, with a truly magnificent tail. Bright birds hover here and there, and the whole design twines itself in perfect order about the cushion. Illustration 2, Plate XXVIII., is dated 1652, and the decoration all made with the pins of the period. This is the earliest example of the kind we have come across; it is made of satin, probably once pink, but now much faded. Nature is most cleverly imitated with the round-headed pins of different sizes which trace the entire design, giving an effect scarcely less beautiful than embroidery. This kind of pincushion was made for presentation, to celebrate a birthday or a wedding, and the initials "A. E." are no doubt those of the fortunate person to whom this one was given. It appears to have been handed down with the pins still in their original places, and not one missing. This tells a tale of stately dames in whose lives there was no unseemly rush—plenty of time for the most elaborate toilet, plenty of time to take a pin carefully out of the design on the pincushion and to put it back into its right hole if it proved not quite the size required. How different to the hurried way in which we now snatch a pin from one of our numerous cushions to cover some deficiency in our dress; and if one pin is too big, or too little, how carelessly we throw it aside and seize another, for there is not time to fetch a needle as we rush through life.

An illustration of the spangled pincushion which belonged about 1680 to Charles Sackville, sixth Earl of Dorset, and was made for the spangled bedroom at Knole, is given in Plate XXVIII., Illustration 3. The furniture and bed in this room were given by King James the First, and are covered with red silk ornamented with gold thread and silver spangles. The pincushion is made of white satin, much faded and sadly frayed, showing the white cotton-wool with which it is stuffed. A coronet formed of steel beads and spangles, with the initials " C. D." (Charles, sixth Earl of Dorset), form the central decoration, and there is on either side of these a device in spangles representing a true lover's knot. The spangles are pale green, but it is impossible to say if that was their original colour. A gilt fringe, now very much tarnished, surrounds the cushion, with tassels of the same at each corner.

Plate XXIX. shews a magnificent pincushion of the time of Charles II., and, for all we know to the contrary, may have been used in one of the royal palaces of that " Merry Monarch." It is embroidered in coloured silks and silver purl on white satin, and the more conventional design compared with that of Queen Elizabeth's time claims attention.

In Plate XXX., Illustrations 1 and 2, we find a most curious accessory to the work-table, made use

PLATE XXIX

Embroidery of the time of Charles II

PLATE XXX

1. Carved Bone Cotton-winder and Pincushion combined, of the time of William and Mary. (Height, 6½ in. ; depth, 2¼ in.)

2. Carved Bone Cotton-winder and Pincushion combined, of the time of William and Mary. (Width, 3½ in.)

3. Round Pincushion for suspension from the girdle. (Diameter, 1¾ in.)

*Late 17th century.*

of by ladies in the reign of William and Mary, and called by its present owner "a cotton-winder and pincushion combined." The pincushions, of which not a vestige remains, were placed on the top of the three pedestals, and the figures on each side of the centre figure unscrew at the waist, shewing receptacles for needles, bodkins, &c. Between the centre and side figures in the cross-piece, which appears to hold the three together, are holes which may have held scissors; and at the back of the centre figure there is a place possibly also meant for scissors. The winders appear between the pincushions, and the whole when fastened to the table by a screw at the back must have been very handy.

There is a design behind and above the head of the centre figure, with a cross at the top of it  It is not a monogram, but more in the nature of a crown. The whole is made of bone, the three figures being more polished than the rest, and of a rather deeper yellow tone.

A pretty little round pincushion for suspension from the girdle is shewn in Plate XXX., Illustration 3, and also belongs to the time of William and Mary. It is covered with silver thread and green silk, and mounted in silver.

In the eighteenth century the Jacobite pincushions are of greater interest than any, for the stirring events of 1745 form an exciting chapter in history, and a halo of romantic enthusiasm surrounds everything connected with Prince Charlie. How many rousing tales have been drawn from the career of this young Prince ! Sir Walter Scott himself tells us, in his introduction to *Waverley*, that that novel is founded upon an incident which took place on the morning of the battle

of Prestonpans; he also makes his hero, Edward
Waverley, in speaking of Prince Charlie, use these words,
"A Prince to live and die for." Endless poems and
ballads also take for their theme some daring deed, some
scene of strife or perilous adventure connected with
the Prince's cause. These ballads graphically describe
the turbulent times with which their authors were
surrounded; for, from the moment Prince Charlie
raised his standard in Glenfinnan on August 19, 1745,
till he was defeated and the remnants of his army dis-
persed in the following April at Culloden, his passage
through Scotland and England provided a series of
subjects to the poets and minstrels of those days, which
their environments and training peculiarly fitted them
to express in song. The young Prince had a charming
appearance and pleasing manner, gave many proofs of
good nature, and was capable of facing danger and
aspiring to fame. These qualities fired the ardour of
many faithful friends and followers who braved death
and ruin for his sake. It is well known to this day
that the "yellow-haired laddie" was very popular
with ladies, especially with the ladies of Lancashire,
who seem to have completely lost their hearts to him
as he marched with his army through that country.
These ladies boldly appeared in the streets of Manchester wearing gowns of Scottish tartans and plaids.
The gentlemen also sported tartan waistcoats, whilst
garters, watch-strings, and pincushions gave expression
to their feelings and bore the motto, "God bless P. C.,
and down with the Rump." Hibbert Ware's *History
of the Foundation of Manchester* provides some interesting and amusing details of this period, which
show that the Whigs becoming intolerant of all these
proceedings, meditated putting the dress and manners

PLATE XXXI

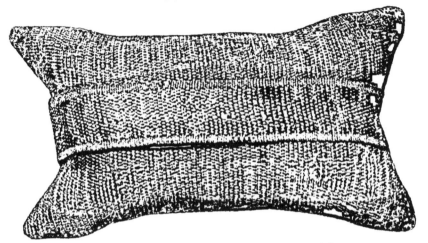

1. Prince Charlie Pincushion.  Size, 3½ in. × 2½ in.

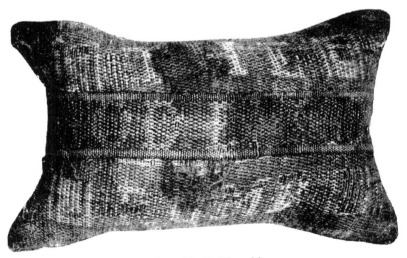

2. Prince Charlie Pincushion.

of the town under the supervision of the police. This gave rise to some humorous hints to the magistrates on the part of the Jacobites, who advised ". . . that a select committee be appointed . . . who have given undeniable proofs of an honest zeal by their regular attendance at bonfires, prosecution of 'Down with the Rumpers', &c. The manufacture committee shall from time to time visit our warehouses, inspect the goods, and severely punish such persons as shall be found to have any which emblematically favour Popery or the Pretender, such as your plaided-chequered gowns, &c., which virtually imply the wearers' approbation of the Scotch Rebellion and the Church of Rome, of which the chris-cross work is a known type or figure. As for your pincushion makers, I think they should be rigorously chastised, and their works publicly burned, let the pretty misses cry as loud as they will. It is a monstrous shame that such an ancient necessary appendage to the ladies' toilet should be thus Jacobitised and transformed from its primitive use into a variegated tool of faction and sedition" Thus we find the pincushion takes its part in the making of history, and at once receives a more important position as having become the innocent cause of much discussion between contending parties. We are pleased to have secured one of these Prince Charlie pincushions (Plate XXXI, Illustrations 1 and 2). It is woven in three colours —blue, yellow, and green—and has a woven band round it. On the band are the words "God bless P. C," and on the pincushion itself we find on one side the words "Down with," and on the other "The Rump."

Where these pincushions were made, and by whom, must be a matter of conjecture; for, being woven, an English loom can hardly have produced them, for they would then have been looked upon as evidence of rank treason.   It is thought possible they came from France, and found their way *via* Scotland to Manchester and other places.   The pincushions were attached to a suspender, by which they must have been hung to a lady's girdle, and worn as a chatelaine, and it is said that many a pretty girl learnt to read "God bless Prince Charlie" upon her pincushion before she could say her catechism.   After the battle of Culloden the bitterness of defeat filled the hearts of the Jacobites, but at the same time inspired them with a noble determination to submit to their fate and make the best of their altered circumstances.   Again, their deepest feelings were expressed in songs and ballads, but these struck a sadder note, and we learn from the strains of forgotten minstrels how heavy with sorrow the hearts of the Jacobites were at this time.   The pincushion, too, had its part to play in these sad scenes, and a touching romance is attached to the one represented in Plates XXXII. and XXXIII., for it bears the names of those who lost their lives for having taken part in the Jacobite rising.

This pincushion is of cream satin printed in dark blue, with four rows of the names of men who died for Prince Charlie and the Jacobite cause. These are arranged on four circles round a central space which is printed with an outlined conventional rose.   Round this rose are the words "Mart. for K. and cou." (Martyr'd for King and country), and the date 1746.   On the obverse side are the names of the leaders and generals (Kilmarnock, Derwentwater, Lovat, and Balmerino, &c.), as well as those of the men.   On the reverse side are seen those

PLATE XXXII

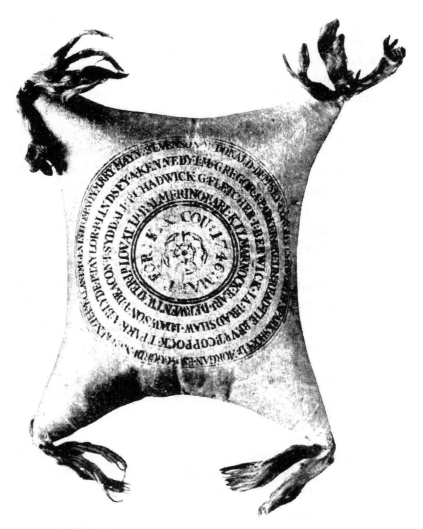

59A.   Jacobite Pincushion shewing the names of the Leaders, Generals, and Men who died for Prince Charlie and the Jacobite cause.

(Size, 3½ in. × 3 in.)

PLATE XXXIII

598.   Jacobite Pincushion shewing the names of the Esquires and Captains
who died for Prince Charlie and the Jacobite cause.

of the esquires and captains. The tassels at the four corners are dark blue.

Another of these interesting relics, similar to that shewn in Plates XXXII and XXXIII., but, alas, in the last stage of decay, was found in repairing the oak-room at Bampton Deanery House, Oxon, together with a deal box containing a hen's egg, upon which was written, "God bless King James III." Inside the box was also a paper inscribed, "I put this in with a designe not to oppen itt till King James comes to the crowne, and I will cape my word itt is a hen's egge, and some of Martha Frederick's haire and her Mother's haire in this Box. I will for ever stick to my principles. I will ever honour my King as long as I live. Martha Frederick." On the back of the paper was written," Do not open this peaper for fere of yr. eyes, for it will blind you"; and on the lid of the box, "It is a forfit to open this box, for it is congering in it and will eat out yr. eyes " It appears that Bampton Deanery House was at one time the residence of two old maiden ladies named Frederick, who left it, towards the close of the eighteenth century, to their kinsman, Edward Frederic Whitaker, Esq. The Whitaker family is now extinct at Bampton.

The awful warning placed upon the lid of this box would effectually prevent its being opened, especially at a time when so many things were shrouded in superstitious mystery, from which the veil has now been lifted.

This relic, which can hardly be touched lest it fall to pieces, is now jealously guarded in the Ashmolean Museum at Oxford. It seems strange that a pincushion should have been chosen as a memorial to those brave men who died for Prince Charlie and for that ancient

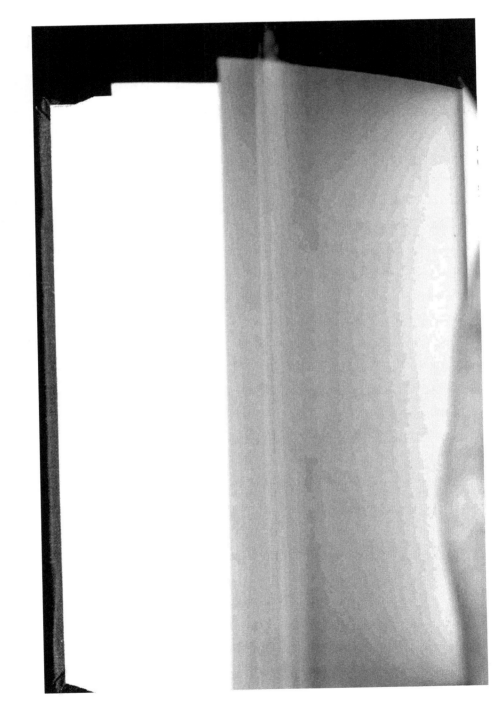

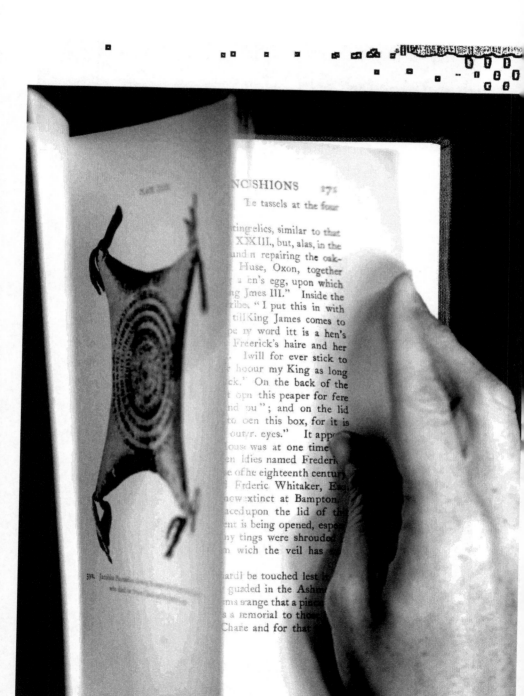

line of kings towards whom there is still a leaning in some parts of Scotland; but that such names as Kilmarnock, Derwentwater, Balmerino, and Lovat should be inscribed upon one does the pincushion much honour, for these gentlemen gave up their lives with gallant courage, thus earning for themselves the right to be enrolled amongst the heroes of history.

Plate XXXIV., Illustration 1, shews the pincushion in rather a novel position between and below two pockets which hang from the waist on to the hooped petticoat of this lady's magnificent costume. The doll was given to Mariana Davis in Paris in 1747, when she was three years old and had just recovered from a dangerous illness. The costume no doubt gives a faithful representation of the Parisian fashions of that day, and we hope Mariana was able to appreciate her valuable possession. But, from the excellent preservation of the dress and all its decorations, we think this doll must have been kept in the drawing-room, and can never have received the extravagant affection so often lavished upon those battered or legless heroines that sleep in the loving arms of many a little child. The doll is two feet high, and made of wood. The dress, which is lifted to shew the pincushion on the petticoat, is of red, white, and green striped silk, with a Watteau back. The petticoat is wide and hooped, and has two pockets suspended from the waist; one has a monogram embroidered on it, and the other a coat of arms. The pincushion is also suspended from the waist by a ribbon strap, and hangs quite low down on the edge of the petticoat. It is covered with satin, of a salmon-pink shade, with a yellowish ground, but the satin is so faded it is impossible to say what the original colours were.

PLATE XXXIV

1. Pincushion hanging from the Waist on to the Skirt of a Doll.
(Size, 2 in. × 1¼ in.   Doll, 2 ft. high.)
1746.

2. Venetian Pincushion.
(Size, 11¼ in. × 8½ in.)
18th century.

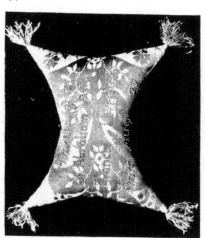

3. Birthday Pincushion.
(Size, 7½ in. × 5 in.)
1751.

Plate XXXIV. gives us in Illustration 2 a Venetian pincushion, which carries our thoughts right away to that enchanting city which rests like a dream upon the bosom of the Adriatic Sea, a vision of surpassing beauty, where all is fair and bright, except, perhaps, the smells and the steamers, which are horrid! But the pins—how glorious they are, their glass heads all glistening with prismatic colours! and how hard it is to pass and repass those gaily decorated shops without running in to buy just one more pin or necklace for some one left behind under the cold grey skies of England. Many little gifts are bought for friends we do not often remember, but think of now only as being old or sad, for the sunshine and the dazzling beauty of this entrancing spot soften our hearts to all the world, and the spell of Venice is upon us, a memory that can never fade. But to return to the pincushion, which is covered with blue-grey figured velvet on a yellow foundation, and has yellow and cream silk tassels, with a border of silver braid. From what piece of costly material can it have been cut? It may have had a glorious past, for we know that in those days, when the pride of Venice was its wealth, magnificent tapestries, carpets, and curtains of velvet, satin, and cloth of gold floated from the windows and balconies of palaces at all State functions or water fêtes. This little piece that now covers the pincushion may have floated with these, or it may have had an even prouder position as part of the state robes of some great Doge, who, with the vestments of his office, wore the ducal crown and its circlet of gold, the historical corno.

The possibilities are great but most uncertain, and we know not what strange scenes of joy or sorrow this silent pincushion may have witnessed; for the pins are gone, and no wonder—the pincushion is stuffed with straw! What self-respecting pin could stand that?

Pincushions decorated entirely with pins seem to have been more or less the fashion for more than two hundred years. In England we find them in 1652 (see Plate XXVIII., Illustration 2), and about a hundred years later, in 1751. The next are dated 1768 and 1794, and the latest we have seen in this style were made in 1830 and 1844. No doubt, when pins became plentiful and more generally used, the idea of decorating pincushions with them instead of with needlework proved a novel and attractive idea, and must have been hailed with delight by many ladies whose fingers were not sufficiently dexterous to admit of their working elaborate designs with a needle, but who had, all the same, enough patience and accuracy of eye to stick pins into a drawing which was not necessarily of their own design. We have already remarked that these pincushions were made to commemorate important events in the lives of our forefathers, such as weddings, and birthdays (see Illustration 3, Plate XXXIV.), made of yellow damask, with gold tassels, round-headed pins forming the words and the dates. They were also a very usual present to a mother with a young baby, in the eighteenth and nineteenth centuries.

Various designs, initials, dates, and appropriate verses were stuck in with pins. Plate XXXV., Illustration 1, a painted cream satin pincushion, with date 1768 and the words " Luck in a Lad " set out in pins, and knotted tassels at each corner, is of particular interest, as it has been used for several generations

PLATE XXXV

1. Maternity Pincushion.
(Size, 6½ in. × 5 in.)
1768.

3. Maternity Pincushion.   (Size, 6½ in. × 4½ in.)
1830.

2. Maternity Pincushion from Camilla
Lacey.   (Size, 7½ in. × 6½ in.)
1794.

4. Wedding Pincushion.   (Size, 7½ in. × 6½ in.)
1840.

with a table-cover to match, both of which were placed upon a table just before the birth of a child in the family of Mascie Taylor of Lymme Hall, Cheshire. The words "Luck in a Lad," formed with pins upon the cushion, express a hope that the expected child will be a boy. It is stuffed with flannel. Another very interesting pincushion of this kind (Plate XXXV, Illustration 2) is kept at Camilla Lacy, near Dorking, in the Burney parlour, and was used at the birth of a son to M. and Mme. d'Arblay (née Fanny Burney) in 1794. It is in white silk, and has the words "Long live the dear child" and five hearts traced in pins on one side   On the other side (shewn in Illustration 2) the pins form the name "F. d'Arblay," surrounded with a decoration made also with pins. Illustration 3, Plate XXXV, is dated 1830, and is one of the gems of our collection. The decoration is the same, entirely in pins, the arrangement of which is a triumph of skill. A lily and a rose lie upon the cushion of cream-white silk, as though just plucked from the garden, whilst the little sprays on each side can only be forget-me-nots—we almost see their colour. A trimming of narrow silk braid goes all round the cushion, fastened on with round-headed pins. The tassels at each corner are silver   The words set out in pins are as clear as printing and most suitable to the occasion, more especially as they are from Byron's pen, which crowns the interest ; for the pincushion was presented to Mrs. White of The Forest, Notts, when her first child was born in 1830, by her friend and neighbour Mary Chaworth, Byron's "Mary," who, when Byron was but fifteen years old, charmed his heart away, and inspired his third great passion. The pincushion, though much faded, is in good preservation, and every pin in its place.

America has also produced pincushions of this kind, and Mrs. Alice Morse Earle describes one in *Child Life in Colonial Days* which had a flowered vine stuck in with pins, and the words " John Winslow, March 1783. Welcome, little stranger." Another given to a Boston baby while his new home was in a state of siege bore the inscription :—

> "Welcome, little stranger,
> Though the port is closed."

The words were formed by the heads of pins. One, of the early nineteenth century, had these words on it :—

> "Peace, prosperity, and joy
> Attend the little girl or boy"

Another of perhaps a century ago is still decorated with the original pins in verses :—

> "God assist the mother through her danger,
> And protect the little stranger."

Yet another reads —

> "May the dew of heaven shine upon
> The appearing flower."

Plate XXXV., Illustration 4, gives a very pretty example of a white satin pincushion designed for a wedding gift, in the same style as the maternity and birthday pincushions. The words, "May you be happy. Presented by E. Bristow, 1844," are formed with pins on one side, and the initials of the bride and bridegroom appear on the other, with little wreaths of flowers in cross-stitch. The custom of presenting gifts on the occasion of a marriage is an old one, and when this pincushion was made about seventy years ago there was of course far less choice in the way of gifts; the

PLATE XXXVI

1 Wedding Souvenir (Size, 2 in × 2 in ) 1841

2 Wedding Souvenir

3 Memorial Pincushion to the Duke of York (Size, 2 in in diameter) 1827

4 Memorial Pincushion to the Duke of York

requirements of life were fewer, and pincushions being then less numerous, the present was one of greater value and importance than it is now. A pincushion is, however, still a very popular present, and no wedding outfit is thought complete unless it contains three or four. Pins having become indispensable to the comfort, happiness, and harmony of existence, it would surely be tempting Providence, if not indeed courting disaster, to start married life without several pincushions. The bride must have one in her suit-case, another in the small bag she carries on her arm, and two more at least packed away in her big trunks. They will all be well supplied with pins, and we should like by reviving a charming custom to feel that a lasting expression of the good wishes of her friends might be carried away by a young bride in such words as " May you be happy " upon her pincushion. A wedding " souvenir " of a little earlier date is found in Plate XXXVI , Illustrations 1 and 2. It was given to Miss Mary Mordaunt on her wedding-day, April 14, 1841, when she was married to Mr. (afterwards Sir) Thomas Dyke Acland. It is made with two pieces of round card covered with very pale blue watered silk and sewn together. On one side the word " souvenir " and the date and designs are formed with a silver cord, which is sewn on with very fine, almost invisible pale blue sewing silk. In the word " souvenir " one side of each letter has a double cord, which gives them a more solid appearance.

The other side has a very curious design, which it is impossible to decipher, but may have been intended to represent the united initials of the bride and bridegroom. The work is exquisite, and this tiny pincushion must once have formed as dainty

M

a gift as ever a young bride received. But, when our thoughts turn to the loving hands, long since at rest, that fashioned and made use of it, such memories fill us with "a gentle sense of gloom," and with a passing sigh we tenderly cover up and put away this little treasure.

The Duke of York's memorial pincushion (Plate XXXVI., Illustrations 3 and 4) completes the series, and proves that the great events of life and death have all been commemorated on pincushions. It is, however, the only one of this particular kind we have found, excepting, of course, the Jacobite pincushions in memory of the martyrs to that cause. The Duke of York's is a pocket pincushion, made of two rounds of card covered with white satin and sewn together at the edges. On one side is a nicely engraved portrait of the Duke of York within a wreath of bay and oak leaves. Underneath the portrait is the inscription: "Published by R. Millar, 14 Paternoster Row." On the other side is an obituary: "His Royal Highness the Duke of York was born 16th August 1763. In his official capacity as commander-in-chief his Royal Highness exercised the great powers vested in him with that wisdom and discretion which stamps a lasting lustre on his name: under his fostering care a race of heroes have appeared, and the soldiers of Britain are at once the dread and admiration of the world: he was unwearied in works of private benevolence   many a soldier's tear has been wiped away, and many widows and orphans have had their sorrows alleviated by the kind exercise of his philanthropy. In a word, he was the Soldier's Friend. His Royal Highness, after great suffering, died the 5th January 1827, in his 64th year."

PLATE XXXVII

1. Group of Knitted Pincushions.
*18th and 19th centuries.*

2. Knitted Pincushion.
(5¼ in. in circumference.)
1815.

3. Small Knitted Pincushion.
(Diameter, 1½ in.)
*18th century.*

4. Knitted Pincushion.
1797.

The pincushion has a little tab of black ribbon, and is stuck round with old black pins.

The group of knitted pincushions in Plate XXXVII, Illustration 1, belong to Mrs. Head, and she says in an article which appeared with them in the *Queen* of 7th March 1903, that ". . . they are remarkable as indicating the length of time a particular style of pattern remained in vogue. All five are made in exactly similar fashion, to wit, knitted in round sections, which are sewn together over a tightly stuffed ball-cushion. The join is hidden by a flat hand-plaited cord of silks similar to those used for the cushion cover, and a length of the same is attached to the top and finished off with a loop, by means of which it was suspended to the waist-belt. The cushion at the top of the plate is the oldest, bearing the date 1782, and the pattern is knitted in dull gold silk on a mulberry ground. The design on the reverse side is a quaint one of two conventional birds facing each other. Next in age to 'S. B.'s' cushion comes 'S. F.'s,' on the left hand, dated 1798, and knitted in brownish purple on white. The reverse is adorned with the moral axiom, 'Let virtue be your guide.' The third cushion—lowest of all—is a bright and pretty tri-coloured affair, striped cream, chocolate, and sky-blue, the lettering and date, 'A present from Ramsgate, 1802,' being in white on the blue, and chocolate on the white stripes Of the two remaining cushions, the large centre one is the clumsiest of all, for it is knitted with harsh crewel-wool, red and white on a green-blue ground It bears signs of having been roughly cut open, perhaps to ascertain whether a banknote or some similar treasure was concealed within, as I believe this idea was responsible for the destruction of a good many of these funny old ball-cushions. This wool-cased example is initialled 'M. W.,' and dated 1817. The last of the five, on the right hand of 'M. W.'s' cushion, is of much later date, yet were it not for the tell-tale '1840' it might be contemporaneous with the first cushion described, so alike are they, especially as regards the patterns on the reverse."

The possibility of exciting discoveries, such as those suggested by Mrs. Head, being connected with knitted pincushions adds greatly to their interest, though we trust the chance of finding hidden treasures will not lead to the ruin of them all. That would be sad indeed, for, alas, how many relics of the past are gradually disappearing. A terrible time called "spring-cleaning" is answerable for much; as surely as each year that season returns, the spirit of destruction invades the hearts of housekeepers, turning many a really charming woman into a destroying angel, as she sweeps away without remorse treasures touched by a thousand memories.

If we now look at Illustration 2 on the same plate, with initials and date 1815, made by Elizabeth Orton, who lived all her life at Swaffham in Norfolk, we shall at once perceive that it is in much better preservation than the centre one of Mrs. Head's group, though made two years earlier. The reason of this may be that so far it has not been suspected of containing anything of value; its form has therefore not been tampered with. Illustration 3 is a pretty example of very fine knitting in brown and white silks, with squared floral forms and the name "C. Osboldestone" set in octagonal spaces; and Illustration 4 excites interest as having belonged to Isabel Strange, whose

PLATE XXXVIII

2. Cornucopia Pincushion. Size, 3 in. and ⅛ × 2 in. and ⅞.
*Early 19th century.*

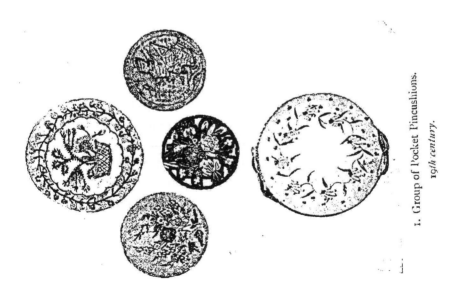

1. Group of Pocket Pincushions.
*19th century.*

initials appear upon it, and who was the wife of Sir Robert Strange, the engraver. The pincushion is knitted in black and white silks, and the twisted cord from which the cushion is suspended is also a mixture of black and white.

Mrs. Head's pocket pincushions (Plate XXXVIII., Illustration 1), displayed in a group, are very dainty and pretty, and must have taken a long time to make. Such fine work could not have been done in a hurry, and would require young eyes and fingers, but the patience of more advanced years. Mrs. Head herself gives a delightful description of this group, which she has kindly allowed us to make use of.

"The pocket pincushions date from rather further back in the nineteenth century than the reign of Queen Victoria. The centre one, at any rate, has a definite history which proves it to be at least eighty years old. Like the four surrounding it, it is made of two circles of card neatly covered and oversewn together, the covering of this particular cushion being deep purple satin, and its diameter just under two inches. Its decoration consists of a bunch of flowers executed in ribbon embroidery, a type of ornamental needlework which has been revived over and over again during the last 150 years. China ribbons—pink, crimson, green, and pale blue—are used, and each wee rose and bud is a mass of the most minute and fairylike quillings. The stems and veinings are put in with stitches of fine green silk. Another example of ribbon-work, in this case combined with beads, is to be seen in the cushion to the left of the centre one, than which it is probably rather older. The covering material is satin, once white, now much time-stained, and the three largest flowers in the gracefully drawn little

M 2

bouquet are worked in pale blue and amber ribbons, but the small forget-me-nots—if so they be—are formed of tiny beads, opaque pink and white and clear glass mixed, while the leaves and stems are done in floss silk of various shades of green. When the pincushion was new it must have been a very bright and delicate affair. At the top of the group is a pincushion covered with white silk, round the edge of which is a wreath of flowers worked in beads of many hues, sprouting at regular intervals from a stem of green silk, each flower consisting of a ring of six to eight threaded beads sewn round a centre one. In the middle of the cushion initials appear to have been worked, but these have been picked out—when, who shall say?—and the ensuing marks concealed by the addition of a delightful old "watch-paper," such as was used between the double cases of ancient watches. This is a circlet of white satin, neatly scalloped and overcast round the edge, and embroidered in the centre with a little basket of flowers in pink and green silks.

"The lowest of the five cushions is larger than the rest, measuring nearly $3\frac{1}{4}$ inches across. It is, moreover, a double one, with leaves of flannel for needles inserted between the two sections. The wreath that adorns its cream-silk covering is prettily worked in opaque blue and clear amber beads, except the connecting leaves, which are lightly painted with watercolour. The reverse is decorated with a wreath of foliage entirely painted. Some of the old hand-made pins, with rolled wire heads, still remain in this cushion. The fifth and last specimen shewn is not embroidered, but covered with white satin, on which maps of Scotland and Ireland are printed and delicately hand-

PLATE XXXIX

1. Heart-shaped Kitchen Pincushion.
(Size, 6 in. × 6 in. in broadest part.)

*Early 19th century.*

2. Heart-shaped Pincushion, decorated
with Beads and Pins.   (Size, 3¾ in. ×
3 in. in broadest part.)

3. Soldier's Pincushion, decorated with Beads and Pins.   (Size, 8 in. from
point to point.)

*19th century.*

coloured. Similar maps are sometimes met with mounted on needlebooks and cases for court plaster."

One word must be said about Illustration 2, Plate XXXVIII., a cornucopia pincushion which is a perfect little gem more than a hundred years old, and yet as fresh and pretty as ever. The details of flowers and fruit are most beautiful, and the whole glowing with colour. It is made of two pieces of cardboard, covered and sewn together. The horn is of cream silk, the shading painted in water-colours, and the back is of mauve silk, quite plain and undecorated. The top of the cornucopia is entirely covered with bead-work, representing bunches of purple grapes, pink roses, and blue, yellow, and white flowers with leaves, the whole of which appear to grow out of the cornucopia. There is a little silk stitching in the gaps between the bead ornaments, which forms a groundwork to the whole, or is, perhaps, also meant to represent the smaller leaves of the flowers. The whole is quite flat, and the pins, some of which are missing, are mostly round-headed.

In Plate XXXIX., Illustration 1, we find the heart-shaped kitchen pincushion which Mrs. Head tells us was in vogue some hundred years ago. It is covered on one side with black velvet and on the other with red merino, the whole surrounded with a ruche of scarlet braid. It is by no means perfect in shape, and a rusty bit of tape remains at the top to hang it up by. It may be thought strange that so romantic a shape should have been chosen for the kitchen. But we all know that romance creeps in there, as into every other place—cooks have many lovers! It may, perchance, be cupboard love sometimes, but not always, by any means. Who can forget the romance of Miss Matty's "capable kitchen," with "such good dark corners," where Martha was unable at first to receive her lover, Jim Hearn, on account of Miss Matty's horror of "followers," and because she had given her word, and would keep it. And when, at Mr. Holbrooke's death, the romance of Miss Matty's own youth, long past but not forgotten, was over, who can forget the touching words with which she gave Martha leave to entertain some "respectable young man" once a week in the kitchen, adding in a low voice, "God forbid that I should grieve any young hearts!" No one who has loved Miss Matty and remembers this little scene can ever say a heart-shaped pincushion is out of place in the kitchen. We might tell other tales of kitchen lovers, not forgetting the proverbial policeman, but such vulgar material would desecrate the memory, all fragrant with lavender and rose leaves, of dear Miss Matty; so we will pass on to Illustration 2, Plate XXXIX., which is not only heart-shaped, but the principal part of the decoration is also heart-shaped, a heart upon a heart. The smaller heart is formed upon the cushion itself with beads, each bead, and here and there a sequin, being held on by a pin. The loop at the top is of red worsted, and was fixed before the cushion was finally sewn up. This is in reality part of the paraphernalia of "heart magic," to which we have already made reference in our second chapter. It still exists in many forms, and is a survival of the use of hearts as charms against those demons who were formerly believed to be the cause of storms and tempests. Sailors, when starting on a voyage, are still often given, for luck, heart-shaped pincushions stuck

full of bead-headed pins in fancy designs, of which
this illustration represents a specimen.

The "Soldier's Pincushion," Illustration 3, Plate
XXXIX , was made after the Crimean War in 1856.
It was not for the use of soldiers, and can hardly
have been used by any one as a pincushion, for the
whole is decorated with beads, and each bead is held
in its place with a pin (as in the heart-shaped pincushion, Illustration 2). It cannot have been made
by an ordinary soldier, and is most likely the work of an
army tailor, for it will be noticed that the diamond-
shaped segments are equally cut and well fitted,
and the material and colours are those used in the
tailoring department of the service. The pincushion
was bought from a soldier, and was probably made
in the first place to kill time, and secondly to take
home as a present to a friend.

After the battle of Waterloo, when at length the
echoes of war with France, which had naturally
exercised a very depressing influence on the nation,
died away, and things in general began to look
brighter, there was a great improvement in many
kinds of workmanship. It is thought probable that
this improvement was partly due to the influence of
those French prisoners who remained in England and
taught the English to make many dainty and pretty
little articles This is not unlikely, for there never
have been people to equal the French in the manufacture of what is new and dainty. Nations, like
individuals, in their intercourse are great imitators;
and the English no doubt were also taught by this
French influence to recognise the advantage of turning
their own talents to account. Improvements of this
kind, though seemingly small, often assist in the general

development of a country. That there was a change
for the better when the war with France and its con-
sequences had passed away seems to be the general
opinion. This may help us to date the pincushions in
Plates XL and XLI. Though it is difficult to speak
with any certainty, we must be guided by the work
itself, bearing in mind that, as a rule, more refinement
was shewn in the workmanship of articles made after
1815–16. Some of the pincushions already mentioned belong to this period; for instance, a few of
the knitted ones and those commemorating births,
weddings, and deaths; but we have thought it better
to place all pincushions of one kind together, irre-
spective of dates, and these last remarks about the
work done during the first half of the nineteenth
century apply more particularly to the bone and ivory
articles that were carved or turned, and it was in this
kind of work that we think the French influence
was mostly felt.

In Plate XL., Illustration 1, a square pincushion
with velvet top, and yellow cord round it, decorated
on each side in white and green silks, is dated
about 1809–10. The pin-tray shewn in Illustration 2, with silver wire twisted in and out of the
pins which form a stand for the tray, is of the same
date; as well as Illustration 3, which can be fastened
by a screw to the table, and was used for holding
needlework whilst it was being done. The little bead
pincushion, Illustration 4, is also dated 1809–10.
Illustrations 1, 2, 3, 4, and 5, Plate XLI., are carved
and pierced bone-work, all about the same date, 1816
to 1818, and we consider them to be specially the
work of the French prisoners or their pupils.

The sign of the Pincushion Inn (Plate XLII.,

PLATE XL

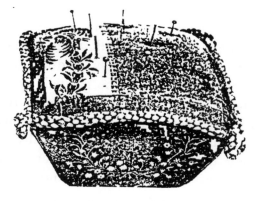

1 Square Pincushion with Velvet Top
(Size, 4⅞ in. square at top, 2½ in. square at base, 2¼ in. deep)
1809-10

2 A Pin Tray
(Size, 4½ in. × 3 in. × 2 in. deep)
1809 10

3 Pincushion to be fastened
to a Table with a Screw
(Size of Pincushion,
2 in. × 1 in.) 1809 10

PLATE XLI

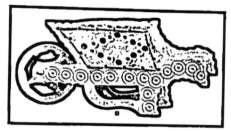

1  Carved and Pierced Bone-work Pincushion
(Size, 2¼ in × 1½ in )
1816-18

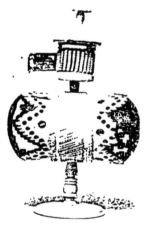

2  Carved and Pierced Bone-work   At
the top a cylinder with a silk
measure enclosed   (Size, 1½ in ×
2½ in )
1816-18

3  Carved and Pierced Bone-
work (Size 2¼ in × 1½ in )
1816-18

4  Carved Bone-work   (Size,

5  Carved Bone-work   (1½ in

PLATE XLII

1. Sign of the Pincushion Inn at Wyberton, near Boston, Lincs.

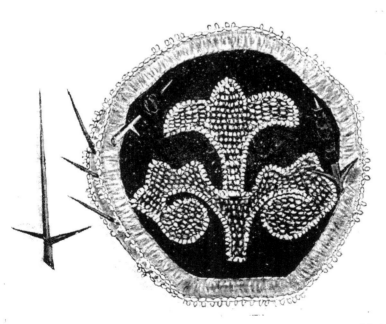

2. Pin-case of the Musquakie Indians of North America. (Size, $3\frac{3}{4}$ in. × $3\frac{3}{4}$ in.)

PLATE XLIII

Pincushion used by Queen Victoria in the Robing-room of Westminster
Abbey at her Coronation, June 28, 1838.

*Presented to the Marchioness of Normanby, by her Majesty's desire,
from the Duchess of Sutherland.*

Illustration 1) is interesting as being the only one of
that name, and though neither the present inn nor its
sign are of any great age, there is every reason to
believe that there was an inn of the same name on
the same spot two or three centuries ago  Reference
is made to it in the old parish accounts, it is also
mentioned in connection with the riots on the enclosure
of Holland Fen, the most southern of the three
divisions of the County of Lincoln, in 1768, and
many old inhabitants speak of it as existing in their
forefathers' time.  The inn stands on the high road
between Boston and London, just where the old
Roman road from the sea-bank over the fens crosses
the high road at right angles.  The present building
dates about sixty years back  The pincushion upon
the inn-sign is painted red, and has a centre decoration
and border of yellow.  The pins are gold.

The pin-case (Illustration 2, Plate XLII ) of the
Musquakie Indians of North America shews that the
thorn, which was the foundation and starting-point
of all pins, in all ages, in all parts of the world, was
in use ten years ago.  The case is made of black
cloth and the design composed of beads.  It was
made and used by the Musquakie Indians in North
America, and given to the University Museum of
Archæology and of Ethnology at Cambridge in 1901.
The squaws, though as a rule more ready to adopt
new fashions than the men, at that time still clung
to the fashion of using the thorns of the honey-locust
(*Gleditschia triacanthos*) instead of the modern pins of
civilisation.

Last, but not least, we have the honour and
pleasure of shewing (Plate XLIII.) an illustration of
the pincushion used by Queen Victoria on the day of

her coronation, June 28, 1838, in the robing-room at Westminster Abbey. The royal arms are worked in fine lace, with V.R. at the top. On that momentous day, in the midst of a scene of the greatest magnificence, her youthful appearance yet dignified bearing were the admiration of all, and stirred in the hearts of her loyal subjects that loving reverence that never ceased to grow as the years rolled on. We are told that when the Queen arrived at the Abbey there was much to be done in the robing-room; it was then the pincushion played its part, and without doubt some of the pins went with her Majesty into the Abbey, and could tell many tales of that thrilling moment when, as the crown touched her royal head, every one shouted for joy, and from the organ burst forth in swelling tones, " God Save the Queen."

THE END

Printed by BALLANTYNE, HANSON & Co
Edinburgh & London

Lightning Source UK Ltd.
Milton Keynes UK
UKHW020655290721
387974UK00007B/901